BROKEN
Vessels

RESTORING BROKEN PASTORS
FOR KINGDOM USE

MARK DENISON, D.MIN.

Broken Vessels
Mark Denison

Published by Austin Brothers Publishing, Fort Worth, Texas
www.abpbooks.com
Author's Website: www.TheresStillHope.org

Copyright 2022 by Mark Denison

The copyright supports and encourages the right to free expression. The purpose is to encourage writers and artists to continue producing work that enriches our culture.

Scanning, uploading, and distribution of this book without permission by the publisher is theft of the author's intellectual property. To obtain permission to use material from the book (other than for review purposes) contact terry@abpbooks.com.

ISBN: 978-1-7375807-4-4

Cover Design: Design Stash - designstashbooks@gmail.com

Printed in the United States of America
2022 -- First Edition

Contents

INTRODUCTION	1
HOW BAD IS THE PROBLEM?	5
WHY DO PASTORS STRUGGLE?	15
CAN YOU LOVE PORN AND GOD?	25
WHO CAN YOU TELL?	37
ARE YOU DISQUALIFIED FROM MINISTRY?	47
FOUR STEPS TO FREEDOM	59
TOOLS YOU CAN USE NOW	69
THE ROAD BACK	77
EIGHT GUARDRAILS THAT WORK	87
AVOIDING RELAPSE	103
A WORD TO THE CHURCH	113
OUR STORIES	123
CONCLUSION	155
NOTES	157
ABOUT THE AUTHOR	173

INTRODUCTION

"All these pieces
Broken and scattered
Mended and whole
Empty handed
But not forsaken
I've been set free
I've been set free."

- Broken Vessels
By Hillsong, 2014

Paul wrote to the church, "We have this treasure in earthen vessels, that the exceeding greatness of the power may be of God, and not from ourselves" (2 Corinthians 4:7 ASV).

The apostle was speaking of the gospel, which he saw as a *treasure*. God has passed on this amazing treasure—the truth of his redeeming love—to all humanity. But it is the conduit of that treasure that is so baffling.

The coin collector stores his gems in a secure safe. The jeweler spends thousands of dollars on cameras and armed security. The need to protect valuables in transport is confirmed by the 13,000 Brink's vehicles in daily operation. People pay Brink's and their 60,000 employees over $4 billion to guard their valuables every year.[1]

So how did God decide to transport his greatest treasure? Paul says that not only did God decide to use "jars of clay" (NIV), but these vessels are "earthen." These were common in the ancient world. As opposed to metal, these clay containers were not considered durable. They were inexpensive and held virtually no intrinsic value.

No one would ever transport his valuables in such vessels. No one except God, that is. God has, in his infinite wisdom, directed that his great treasure would be left in the hands of the most brittle of all possible containers. The earthen vessels could hardly be counted on to carry the treasure a great distance. Yet, God has trusted his children to transport the good news to the darkest corners of creation.

God chose to use earthen vessels, knowing that they did not merely carry the potential for breakage, but the guarantee. He knew that we would become *broken vessels* by the time our assignment was due. Let me say it like this:

God doesn't just use broken vessels. *God only uses broken vessels*. There is no other kind.

Let's unpack the numbers. One estimate concludes that there are 327,515 ordained ministers in the United States.[2] Other estimates put the number at 600,000 clergymen.[3] These ministers are serving approximately 380,000 churches in the U.S.[4] And given the estimate that 37 percent of pastors are viewing pornography,[5] that puts the number of ministers hooked on porn in America somewhere between 120,000 and 222,000.

It is more difficult to quantify actual addiction. I like the definition of sexual addiction first proposed by Gerald May in *Addiction and Grace*.[6] May defines addiction as "a state of compulsion, obsession, or preoccupation that enslaves a person's will and desire." But don't be confined by this definition. Any use of porn or sex outside of marriage is dangerous.

And any use of porn renders the pastor a broken vessel.

When Gideon went to war with the Midianites, he took 100 men with him. The men were equipped for battle with two "weapons"—trumpets and jars (vessels). When the moment of truth came, when they confronted the enemy, the men were told to do two things: blow your trumpet and shatter your vessels. The men obediently "smashed the jars" (Judges 7:20).

Not only does God use broken vessels, he sometimes breaks the vessels himself. It is in our brokenness that we are made useful to the Master.

Broken Vessels

The central question with which we will wrestle throughout this book can be settled before the first chapter.

Can God use a pastor who has fallen, who is broken, and who has sinned?

A better question would be whether God can use anyone who is not a broken vessel. The evidence is in.

Pastor, when you were called to ministry, a foundation of that call was surely that you would maintain godly character. It was always your goal to live a life worthy of your call. That is commendable.

But now you have fallen. That pure vessel through which God once ministered so powerfully has been broken. I get it. I've been there. *I'm still there.*

The time for your pity party is over. The time for self-condemnation has passed. The time to listen to your critics is done.

Can God use you again, pastor? To say no is to elevate the power of your sin above the power of the cross. God can use broken vessels. God does use broken vessels. God must use broken vessels.

God *only* uses broken vessels.

This book is not for those who have not yet been broken. They are not yet of their greatest use. This is for those who have been broken, shattered, and devastated. They are in exactly the right place to get back into the game. Pastor, your best work is just ahead.

Welcome to the cherished club of the broken vessels.

Chapter 1
HOW BAD IS THE PROBLEM?

The world is flat. It snows a lot in Florida. I will be the next point guard for the Los Angeles Lakers. Pornography isn't a problem among Christians.

By comparison to the last statement (porn isn't a problem among Christians), the first three proclamations are completely rational.

I'm guessing I don't have to convince you there is a porn problem today. But I'm going to do it anyway. Get ready for a tsunami of evidence to support my presupposition. What we are facing today is a porn revolution unseen in human history. And sadly, the revolution that once knocked on the door of the local church has now kicked that door in. Jimmy Draper, retired president of *LifeWay*, said it well: "It appears the sin of choice among Christians today is pornography."[1]

In 2018, Josh McDowell spoke at the *Reasonable Faith Conference* in Singapore. He stated, "The problem is that 98 percent of pastors in the world are not equipped to help anyone deal with their porn addiction. If they did, they wouldn't have time to do anything else." [2]

While the focus of this book is to address the effect of porn on pastors, I will first lay out the magnitude of the porn epidemic in general, then in the pew and finally the pulpit.

General Porn Data

Hugh Hefner published the first edition of *Playboy* in December 1953 with a picture of Marilyn Monroe on the cover. But let's be clear. Sex addiction predates *Playboy*. In fact, there are some sex addicts who have *never* viewed pornography. And our interest here is with the broader issue of sexual addiction, rather than just pornography, per se. But we will confine most of our discussion on the porn issue specifically, for two reasons.

First, most sex addicts are porn addicts.

Second, documentation of porn use is much more accessible—and reliable—than data on other forms of sexual addiction. So let's begin our discussion with general data on porn use.

- In 2020, porn sites received more traffic than Twitter, Instagram, Netflix, Zoom, Pinterest, and LinkedIn combined.[3]
- A 2015 meta-analysis of 22 studies from seven countries found that the consumption of porn was significantly associated with increases in sexual aggression.[4]
- A United Kingdom survey found that 44 percent of males ages 11–16 who had consumed porn reported that online porn gave them ideas about the type of sex they wanted to try.[5]
- In 2019, the equivalent of nearly 6,650 centuries of porn was consumed on one of the world's largest porn sites.[6]
- The world's second largest free porn site received 42 billion visits in 2019.[7]
- Sixty-four percent of youth pastors and 57 percent of pastors struggle with porn.[8]
- Pornhub, the world's most popular porn website, reported the following in 2017: 28.5 billion annual visits to their site, 81 million daily visits, 25 billion searches performed, 50,000 searches per minute, 800 searches per second, 4,052,542 videos uploaded, and 68 years' worth of content uploaded.[9]
- The average visit to a porn site lasts 6.5 minutes.[10]
- Pornhub reported, in one year: 3,732 petabytes of information transmitted—enough to fill the memory of every iPhone on Earth.[11]

Internet Porn Revenue

A good snapshot of the magnitude of the porn industry is a brief review of the money spent on this addiction. The dollars spent across the globe every second of every minute are of staggering proportions. The numbers are as mind-boggling as trying to grasp the national debt. But the data are informative.

- Webroot Cybersecurity reports that 28,258 users are watching porn every second, at a cost of $3,075.64 every second.[12]
- In six years, the porn industry grew from a $1 billion industry to a $3 billion industry.[13]
- Online porn subscriptions exceed $2.8 billion per year.[14]

The Effects of Porn on Marriage

We hear it a lot in our ministry: "Porn isn't a problem for our marriage." Another myth is that a man can have a porn addiction without having an affair. *Porn use is an affair.* Of course, most porn users must justify their behavior in order to look in the mirror every day. Nothing is more minimized than the disastrous effects of porn, especially on a marriage. Following are several pieces of direct evidence that porn does, indeed, ruin marriages.

- Sociologist Jill Manning has found that porn consumption is associated with increased marital stress, decreased marital intimacy and sexual satisfaction, infidelity, increased appetite for more graphic types of porn, devaluing of monogamy, and sexual addiction.[15]
- According to the *Journal of Adolescent Health*, prolonged exposure to porn leads to: diminished trust between husband/wife, abandonment of the hope of sexual monogamy, belief that promiscuity is normal, belief that abstinence is unhealthy, belief that marriage is sexually confining, lack of attraction to family and child-raising.[16]
- A survey by the American Academy of Matrimonial Lawyers reported the following factors in divorce: 68

percent had one partner meeting a new lover on the Internet, 56 percent had one partner with an "obsessive interest in pornographic websites," 47 percent had one partner spending excessive time on his computer, and 33 percent were involved in chat rooms.[17]

Porn Use and Generation Z

The first generation with a famous tag line was the Baby Boomers, born 1946–1964. This post-World War II generation was followed by Generation X, consisting of people born from 1965–1980. Then came Gen Y, those born roughly from 1981–1996. These are also referred to as the Millennial Generation.

But now we have Gen Z, those born from the late 1990s through today (2022). For our purposes, we will focus on those whose ages are 13–19. Back in "my day," we simply called these "teenagers," then "youth," and finally "students." Our question here is this: What effect is pornography having on this generation?

- Josh McDowell has found that 57 percent of teens seek porn at least once a month.[18]
- One study found that 32 percent of boys and 18 percent of girls have viewed bestiality online; 18 percent of boys and 10 percent of girls have viewed rape or other types of sexual violence; and 15 percent of boys and nine percent of girls have watched child pornography online.[19]

Internet Porn and Young Adults

No generation is exempt from the dangers of porn. The young adult group is key, in that they are the emerging leaders across the globe. Even a cursory look at the magnitude of porn use on college campuses should haunt any of us who know what a life embedded in porn from young adulthood can look like.

- A study of 813 students from six U.S. universities found that 66.5 percent of college men and 48.7 percent of col-

lege women find viewing pornographic materials to be an acceptable way to explore one's sexuality, and 21.3 percent of college men admitted to viewing porn every day, while only 13.9 percent say they never view porn.[20]
- Another survey of 29,000 college students concluded that 42 percent of male students and 20 percent of female students regularly read sexually explicit magazines.[21]

Porn and the Workplace

I'm not much for predictions, but I have one with which I have great confidence. The day will come (sooner, rather than later) when the business community will embrace anything that combats porn use in the workplace. So many hours are lost to porn use in the workplace that business leaders would be prudent to address this pandemic on purely financial grounds, if nothing else.

- A Barna survey found that 63 percent of adult men had looked at porn while at work in a three-month period; 38 percent do so repeatedly. For women in the workplace, those numbers are 36 percent and 13 percent.[22]
- A study of 474 human resource professionals conducted by *Business & Legal Reports* concluded that two-thirds said they have discovered porn on their employees' computers.[23]
- According to a study from 2004, 70 percent of Internet porn traffic occurs between 9:00 a.m. and 5:00 p.m., while most people are at work.[24]

Porn Use Among Church Goers

This is where the evidence becomes especially troubling. As believers, we would like to think that what has ensnared the world has mostly left the Church unharmed. Surely, porn use among believers can't be anywhere nearly as widespread as it is outside the Church, right? Unfortunately, that is not the case. In fact, much evidence suggests porn use among church goers is only negligibly less than among the general population.

- A survey conducted for Proven Men Ministries in 2014 found that porn use among self-identified Christian men was only negligibly better than among non-believers.[25]
- Barna found that 41 percent of practicing Christian boys 13–24 use porn at least once a month, while 23 percent of practicing Christian men 25 and older do the same.[26]
- Another study found that, while regular church attenders are 26 percent less likely to look at porn, those self-described as "fundamentalists" are actually 91 percent more likely to look at porn.[27]
- Marnie Ferree cites a 2006 poll that found 20 percent of Christian women are frequent porn users.[28]
- Sadly, 53 percent of Promise Keeper attendees admitted to using porn the week they attended the conference.[29]

Porn Use Among Pastors

In the following chapters, this is our focus. As the numbers indicate, porn use among clergy is on the rise. There are many reasons for that, which are discussed later. First, it must be established that many pastors have become "broken vessels" due to the use of pornography and sexual brokenness.

- Josh McDowell's *The Porn Phenomenon* includes a survey by the Barna Group in 2016 that found one in five youth leaders and one in seven senior pastors use porn regularly. That comes to 50,000 church leaders. Forty-three percent of pastors say they have at least struggled with porn in the past, and only seven percent of pastors have any kind of program in their church to address the issue of pornography.[30]
- In August 2000, *Christianity Today* conducted an exclusive survey of its readership. They found the following. Eleven percent of the calls received on the Focus on the Family Pastoral Care Line were about pastors and

online porn. One year later, that jumped to 20 percent. Thirty-three percent of pastors admitted to looking at sexually explicit websites, though 30 percent have never told anyone of their struggle.[31]
- In another survey, 43 percent of pastors admit to viewing online porn, 37 percent say it is a "current struggle," and 75 percent have no accountability.[32]

Porn Use and Erectile Dysfunction

Another myth about pornography is that it has no long-term effects on the user. I hear the refrain often: "A little pleasure won't hurt anyone." Actually, it hurts the person engaged in the "little pleasure." Not only do porn and masturbation damage a committed relationship, they damage the person engaging in the behavior. One example, as documented by recent research, is that of erectile dysfunction. The correlation between porn/masturbation and ED is striking.

- A 2015 study of men (mean age of 36) found that frequent use of porn resulted in ED, accompanied by a decreased desire for sex with one's partner.[33]
- Another study concluded that among porn users, 71 percent had sexual dysfunctions.[34]
- A study by Dr. Valerie Voon found that men who engaged in compulsive pornography "had greater impairments of sexual arousal and erectile difficulties in intimate relationships, but not with sexually explicit materials."[35]

Sexting

Sexting is no longer just a young man's "sport." What began largely as an activity for boys has evolved. Now, young girls and adults of both sexes and all ages are engaged in the practice at an alarming rate. Sexting may be the fastest growing problem in the area of sexual addiction. This is especially true among church goers, who erroneously think the privacy of technology provides "cover." It does not!

- A 2018 survey found that 27 percent of teens are sexting.[36]
- A 2017 study found that 99 percent of Americans approve—at least somewhat—of posting explicit pictures online, so long as the person posting the pictures is not in a committed relationship.[37]
- Barna found that 51 percent of porn users also send nude pictures by text or email.[38]
- A survey of 500 teens, ages 13-18, in the UK, found that 60 percent have received requests for nude photos.[39]

Various Correlations of Porn Use

Porn use is never an isolated phenomenon. It has far-reaching impacts in more ways than we can know. None of them are good. We will just scratch the surface here, providing a few examples of the influence of porn on various areas of life. It is important to know that you engage in this behavior today, the impact will be felt tomorrow—and beyond.

- When a child is directly exposed to porn, the following effects have been documented: lasting negative or traumatic emotional responses; earlier onset of sexual intercourse; and a diminished appreciation for marriage.[40]
- When teens are exposed to porn, that leads to frequent cheating on one's partner.[41]
- An extensive study has concluded there is a direct link from porn use to increased loneliness.[42]
- Another study concluded porn use leads to depression.[43]
- A study of 2,305 Dutch adolescents found a correlation between porn use and the belief that women are simply sex objects.[44]
- Men and women who use porn increasingly see relationships as casual rather than committed.[45]
- Thirty percent of porn users admit this has negatively affected their work.[46]

- When adolescents are exposed to pornography, the following effects have been documented: lasting traumatic responses; earlier onset of sexual intercourse; reduced interest in marriage; increased risk for sexual addiction.[47]
- Porn use in young age leads to a greater acceptance of adultery.[48]
- A study of 400 internet users found a significant correlation between pornography use and loneliness.[49]

Pornography and Violence

This may be the most alarming issue with pornography. Increasingly, porn presentations are violent and they lead to violence. To simply look the other way is akin to burying one's head in the sand. If nothing else serves as a deterrent for porn use among the younger generations, this should. The correlation between porn use and violent behavior is unmistakable.

- In a meta-analysis of 46 studies published from 1962 to 1995, with total samples of 12,323 people, it was found that porn use results in the following: 31 percent increased risk of sexually deviant behavior, 22 percent increase in sexual offenses, and 31 percent increase in accepting rape as normal behavior.[50]
- A meta-analysis of 24 studies found a direct correlation between sexual violence and frequent use of porn.[51]
- Adolescent exposure to porn is a reliable predictor of adult sex crimes.[52]
- Arrested prostitution clients are twice as likely to report having watched pornographic movies than those who have not.[53]
- A study of 271 women who were victims of sex offenses found that men who use both porn and alcohol are 3.2 times more likely to commit violent sexual offenses.[54]
- A study of 304 pornographic scenes found that 88.2 percent contained violence.[55]

Summary

By now, it should be clear that we have a huge problem with sex/porn addiction in America and throughout the world. Our ministry has worked with clients in nearly every state and on every continent. The rise in porn use and its devastating results cannot be overstated. But of further concern to our ministry is the impact of the pandemic in the pew and pulpit. I know what it is to be a broken vessel. And I have witnessed firsthand the mending of hundreds of other broken vessels. That the problem is so vast must only serve to challenge our resolve to provide hope and healing for the wounded. It is then that broken vessels are put back together, they become exceedingly useful, and the kingdom's work is expanded.

Chapter 2
WHY DO PASTORS STRUGGLE?

To review, the magnitude of the porn problem in the pulpit is indisputable. Let's revisit the problem by the numbers, as put forth in the previous chapter. You may want to peruse these data points sitting down. Various studies record slightly different statistics, as we will show, but their general findings are consistent.

- One in five youth leaders use porn regularly.
- One in seven senior pastors use porn regularly.
- Forty-three percent of pastors admit to a porn problem in the past.
- Only seven percent of churches address the issue.
- Thirty percent of pastors who struggle with porn never admit it to anyone (meaning they get no help).
- Another study found that 37 percent of pastors say porn is a current struggle.
- Only 25 percent of pastors have any kind of accountability.

As hard as it might be for church members to accept this data, it is even harder for ministers to acknowledge their struggle. Sam Louie writes, "It's hard enough for people in the general population who struggle with sexual or porn-related compulsive behavior to acknowledge the problem, let alone a pastor whose job is to expound on spiritual truths and be a living example of morality above reproach." [1]

Six Challenges Pastors Face

Before delving into specific reasons pastors have a higher-than-expected porn problem, let's provide a macro look at the life of a pastor. It is helpful to identify some of the specific challenges that are unique to ministry. If you have never walked in a pastor's shoes, you will never be able to fully identify with these struggles. Each of these is covered more extensively by Ed Stetzer in an article published in 2019.[2]

1. Pastors struggle with identity.

As a pastor, you need to balance three identities thrust upon you: (a) religious identity, (b) cultural identity, and (c) your own identity. Your community will see you differently than your church, your friends, your wife, or your children.

As a pastor, you are always on display. When you are seen at the ball game, you are viewed as a pastor just as much as if you were in the pulpit at that moment. Most people who call you "Pastor" at the church building will also call you "Pastor" when they run into you at Walmart.

But the fact is, what you do is not who you are. I suppose that this is the space in which I should give you two or three tips on how to escape this identity quagmire. But I honestly never achieved that myself. I still walk with it today. "Once a pastor, always a pastor" is the way many view us. So I still get the calls. Just today (this day of writing), an old friend from my first church, whom I have known since the mid-1980s, texted me a question about the Holy Spirit from Acts 8. And I was happy to respond quickly. And that's healthy—as long as I find my value in being my buddy's friend, whether I'm his pastor or not.

"There is no call higher than to be a pastor." I heard that refrain in seminary nearly every week. But I came to reject that thesis, as I have said yes to a higher call—to simply be a surrendered child of the King.

2. Pastors struggle with community.

Stetzer poses a good question. "How do you get into community with people who either put you too high on a pedestal or watch for your every fault and failure?"[3] The answer is often elusive. Sometimes, we sacrifice our search for community on the altar of convenience. Why? We've been burned too many times.

I've heard so many pastors confess that they aren't really close to anybody. And that's sad. But for many, that is better than being close to the wrong person. We must be careful before divulging our secrets and struggles to someone who has not earned our trust.

In one of my pastorates, I made the mistake of chasing community too fast. I figured I had room for about five close friends from among the men in my church. I basically received the first five men into that circle who tried to get in.

Big mistake.

But there is a mistake that can be just as costly. That is to trust no one. We are not wired to do life—or ministry—alone. Just as Jesus had his inner circle (Peter, James, and John), you need yours. Find them from within your church. Or from outside your church. Just make sure you find them.

3. Pastors struggle with boundaries.

As pastors, we must remember that we cannot have a deep personal relationship with everyone in the church. We want to shepherd them to the degree that we can. If the church is larger, we will usually shepherd them through our teaching during weekend services. Or we will find other ways to utilize our gifts and passions.

But we need to have boundaries and know when to say yes and no. Many feel that they will be condemned if they say no to anything. I get it, as the founding member of the People-Pleasing Pastors Club. But we can't say yes to everything. Sometimes, the best thing we can say is no. In fact, "No" is actually a complete sentence.

Chantelle Pattemore writes, "Boundaries are a way to take care of ourselves. When you understand how to set and maintain healthy boundaries, you can avoid the feelings of resentment, disappointment, and anger that build up when limits have been pushed."[4]

4. Pastors struggle with accountability.

Don't misunderstand. As a pastor, you can't be accountable to *everyone*. But you do need to be accountable to *someone*. For some, accountability is built into the system. Your church may have elders or some other governing board to whom you are accountable.

You will know that you are in a healthy place when accountability is not just something you accept, but becomes something you value. And don't tie correctness to accountability. For example, if you are the discipleship pastor and your senior pastor asks you to implement a new curriculum of which you aren't particularly fond, remember that you don't have to agree with him to follow his leadership.

Accountability can be your best protection. When you visit someone in the hospital, someone needs to know where you are going and when. When you handle church funds, there must be someone else in the room. When you counsel with a woman, your assistant or wife needs to be nearby.

So why do pastors struggle with accountability? Other than nefarious reasons, the pastor may feel like he has all the right answers. Autocratic rule is, after all, very efficient. (*Efficient* does not always mean *successful*.) But the downside of being the lone ranger is too dangerous. Accountability is one of your best friends, whether you embrace it or not.

5. Pastors struggle psychologically.

A Lifeway Research study found that 23 percent of pastors indicated they had struggled with mental illness of some kind.[5] As sad as that is, compounding the problem is that pastors feel like they can't share this struggle, even privately.

My old pastor, Dr. Cecil Sewell, gave me some great advice when I was a young pastor. "Never resign on a Monday," he told me. He continued, "Things at your church are never as good as your best Sunday, nor are they as bad as your worst Sunday." Dr. Sewell's goal was to keep this neophyte pastor on an even keel. (For the most part, I think it worked.)

Through the years, I have known hundreds of pastors, some very well. These are good men. But many are plagued with any number of psychological challenges. They watch Andy Stanley preach, and feel they don't preach well enough. They watch John Piper, and feel they aren't deep enough. And they watch Joel Osteen and feel they aren't happy enough.

Pastors are often eaten alive with feelings of inadequacy and loneliness. They are overworked and underpaid. They can please most of the people some of the time, but can't please any of the people all of the time. It's no wonder so many struggle psychologically.

6. Pastors struggle spiritually.

As a professional minister, it can be challenging to be seen as the voice of God. While others expect us to have all the answers, we know our real job is to point them to the one who really does. The truth is, every pastor knows what it is to struggle spiritually.

We had a guest speaker in seminary one day. He was the pastor of one of the largest churches in America. After his presentation, he fielded questions from the student body. And for every question, he had a quick—and brilliant—response. So long as the subject was evangelism, homiletics, Greek, Hebrew, philosophy, or hermeneutics, he was ready.

Then the mega-church pastor was stumped with a question from a young student. "Can you tell us about your personal quiet time?" The pastor literally said, "I'm not sure what that is."

At the time, a condemning spirit rose up within me. Today, I get it. There are too many days when my personal devotional time is relegated to a quick read of *My Utmost for His Highest*, just so I can check off the box. I'm not good at journaling and I don't meditate enough. My prayers are often too self-centered.

Many of us (not just pastors) struggle in areas that might surprise. My doctor needs to lose weight. My dentist had cavities the last time I asked. My therapist is in therapy and many of my best friends are in denial.

It's not that pastors are *unspiritual*. It's just that we are usually much better at feeding others than feeding ourselves. And if we are honest, we'll admit that being spiritual is sometimes hard work. Otherwise, everyone would do it.

But Why the Porn Problem?

Pastors are perhaps the most susceptible to the attack of porn and sex addiction for several reasons. While it is impossible to identify every contributing factor to porn in the pulpit, several seem obvious.

1. Pastors are the natural target of the enemy.

Satan knows that if he brings down the pastor, he will cripple the church. We can all think of examples where this has proven true. The senior pastor is the most natural target of enemy attack. I once heard an old preacher talk about Satan's attack on pastors. Noting that the enemy sets his eyes on church leaders, the preacher said of Satan, "He wouldn't be much of a devil if he didn't."

2. Pastors live on pedestals.

They enjoy the rush of speaking before large crowds every week (admittedly, captive audiences), hearing lots of praise, and living in an age that has built a wall between clergy and laity. As one speaker said, "The church has sanitized her pastor." It's not that pastors necessarily fall more than others; it is just more noticed, for the higher the pedestal, the greater the fall. One could argue that all public leaders, such as businessmen and physicians, live on a pedestal. But if a business leader uses porn, it is unlikely to cost him his job or reputation. The pastoral pedestal is unlike any other.

3. Pastors isolate.

They have little accountability and spend hours alone, unmonitored, each week. When they "visit the hospitals," no one really knows where they are the entire time. Adding to their isolation is that no one in the church can really understand the pressures a pastor feels until they have been there. His job is never done and the stress is tremendous. That is why, according to Dr. John Bisagno, only one in ten pastors finishes strong. None of this is to say isolation is okay. It's not, but it is understandable.

4. Ministers are relational by nature.

They need to be. But this makes them more susceptible to affairs and inappropriate behavior. Their position and demeanor make pastors more attractive to women than they would otherwise be, as women are largely relationally and emotionally centered. Many ministers enter a danger zone with women without even realizing it. A counseling session, word of encouragement, or even a brief conversation in the halls of the church—they can all be misinterpreted and they can lead to further discussions which become a slippery slope to serious trouble.

5. Pastors receive more criticism than most professionals.

As a result, they become people pleasers. Their drive for approval leads many pastors to indulge in artificial relationships with porn or even prostitutes. These relationships place no demands on the addict, and in that sense, they are safe. The answer is for the pastor to base his self-esteem on the affirmation of his wife and family friends. None of us likes criticism, and I really don't know anyone who takes it well. The key is that the pastor not self-medicate in his effort to blunt the pain that comes with critical words.

6. Pastors feel bulletproof.

Because there is little accountability, the minister can live in his addiction for years without being discovered. And with every passing day, he comes to assume that since he has not been caught, he never will be. "God will protect me," he reasons. Some go so far in their thinking as to assume God is under an obligation to protect them, simply for the sake of the church. Of course, this eventually leads to a monumental fall, as God is under no obligation to protect any of us from our secrets. In fact, it is in our discovery that we can be made whole.

7. Pastors lead an army of volunteers.

Dr. Hershael York, professor at Southern Seminary, observed, "If a businessman has to correct a worker's performance, he has the leverage of a paycheck whose necessity powerfully motivates employees to do what they are asked. Workers in the church, however, do not need the job they perform in order to put food on the table and may even have easier lives without it." [6] Compounding the issue is that in most churches, the majority of volunteers are women. Therefore, a certain amount of time spent with women other than the pastor's wife is almost inevitable.

The Answer

If you are a pastor, it is important that you engage a plan *before* you fall. There is a low tolerance in most churches for pastors who commit the same sins as their parishioners. If you are caught in a porn habit, you probably won't get a second chance. Preventative measures are in order from day one. The following suggestions might help.

1. Recognize your unique challenges.

Max DuPree writes, "The first responsibility of a leader is to define reality."[7] That's where many of us get off the rails. When we begin to play with fire, we don't recognize it. We don't bow to the reality of our situation and temptations. Porn doesn't strike in a vacuum. Porn addictions have as their genesis some level of trauma, abuse, or isolation. If we are to effectively combat our unique struggles, we must first identify them.

The unrealistic expectations hoisted upon the shoulders of pastors will wear most of us down.

Thom Rainer, one of the foremost voices on pastoral leadership today, writes, "Expectations of pastors can be unrealistic. Pastors are often expected to attend multiple meetings, to visit countless congregants, to prepare sermons with excellence, to provide ongoing strategic leadership, to conduct weddings and funerals, and to be involved in the community."[8]

The answer is to recognize the challenges of ministry. Until then, we cannot address these challenges.

2. Keep a therapist on speed dial.

I am grateful for the therapists God has brought into my life through the years. I am especially thankful for the two C.S.A.T.s who guided me through early recovery. I can't recommend seeing a Certified Sex Addiction Therapist enough. They are uniquely qualified to direct you into the liberating pathway of recovery.

We all need therapy from time to time. Even therapists see therapists. It's part of their training.

Dr. Ryan Howes, noted psychologist, author, and professor at Fuller Graduate School of Psychology, underscores this thesis. He writes, "I believe everyone could benefit from some time in therapy or at least getting a mental health checkup at regular intervals in their lives. Your future self would appreciate the foresight of your current self having a screening and establishing an objective baseline of cognitive and psychological functioning."[9]

Therapy is integral to recovery from sexual addictions, but its benefits are far more reaching than that. Darin Shaw, with Honey Lake Clinic near Jacksonville, addresses the need for Christian counseling. "Christian counseling can be a great help in overcoming addictions, dealing with mental health or mood disorders, navigating personal struggles, grief or loss, and healing marital and family issues."[10]

3. Practice rigorous self-care.

I loved every minute of my seminary experience. I have four degrees from Christian universities and seminaries. I was surprised when I added up all the official hours that led to my degrees—298. That's a lot of classwork, papers, lectures, and books. I praise God for my training in theology, church history, preaching, evangelism, leadership, administration, pastoral care, Greek, Hebrew, the Old Testament, the New Testament, and more. But what I don't recall was ever taking a class on self-care.

Caring for others comes naturally for most pastors. The problem is that we don't know when or how to turn it off. Thom Rainer writes, "Many pastors don't know how or when to say 'no.' And many are not good at delegating, or they really don't have anyone who can handle some of their responsibilities."[11]

Effective self-care must address each of the following four areas of life.

- Spiritual. The objective is to find a place apart from the daily grind, where you can get in touch with God and discover who you are within the context of his love.
- Mental. Meditation, reading, and collaboration are all elements of mental self-care. This is a part of psychological integrity and health.
- Emotional. It is important to stay in touch with how you are doing by listening to your feelings, identifying your emotions, and interpreting their meanings.
- Physical. A healthy diet and regular exercise, along with adequate sleep and time to unplug are all effective means to physical well-being.

4. Maintain your spiritual connection.

Nothing should ever come before your connection with God. Let me repeat that. *Nothing should ever come before your connection with God.* That includes your ministry. Everything we do in service to our God must emanate from a heart filled with his presence. Our service to God must never become a substitute for our walk with God.

In maintaining a true, dynamic walk with the God of the universe, we must set all other sources free. Don't ask anyone but God to fill the God-shaped emptiness in your heart. Author and speaker Shana Schutte states, "Having an intimate relationship with God means realizing that abundant life will never be found in another person."[12]

Chapter 3
CAN YOU LOVE PORN AND GOD?

This is a question many of us have wrestled with mightily. In the manmade hierarchy of sin, porn and sexually addictive activities rank near the top, somewhere above lying, profanity, and substance abuse, and only slightly beneath the unpardonable sin. For the pastor, it is deemed far worse to view porn one day than to not have a personal devotion time for a year. We define a person more by what he does than by who he is.

Of course, none of this justifies a single instance of porn use or illegitimate sexual acting out. But that's not the question. Most would agree the sex addict can love God—*apart* from his addiction. But can he love God while still *in* his addiction? The way we answer that as a church means everything. It will determine how we respond to the epidemic that I'm calling "porn in the pew."

While the limitations of this book do not allow for an exhaustive response to "the question," we will briefly address it head-on. *Can you love God and porn at the same time?* I propose six responses that will answer that question.

A Practical Response

Let's answer "the question" with a series of smaller questions. Can a person eat too much chocolate and still love God? Can he play too much golf and still love God? Can a man say something inappropriate and still love God? Did David love God and Bathsheba at the same time? Did Peter love the Lord he denied?

John the Divine made it clear in his first epistle that a man who says he has moved beyond sin is not telling the truth. So whether he mismanages his diet, time, money, speech, or sex drive—all forbidden in Scripture—he is still the same sinner saved by grace. Nelson Mandela said it well. "I am not a saint unless you think of a saint as a sinner who keeps on trying."

Whether a man can view porn without shame is a different topic. Can a man indulge in sexual promiscuity void of shame or conviction, without repentance, while at the same moment embracing an intimate spiritual connection? I think not. But can he still be in the fight of his life, a fight for purity not yet won, and love God? I say yes. In fact, I suggest that if that were not true, that man would have no hope.

A Historical Response

The Apostle Paul wrote, "I do not the good I want to do, but the evil I do not want to do—this I keep on doing" (Romans 7:19). So how is it that the great apostle, clearly in love with God, had an ongoing struggle with sin? Is this a blight on his character? Was he not a man of integrity? How can it be possible that a man sincerely loves and serves God while struggling with ongoing sin? J.I. Packer offers brilliant insight. He said, "Paul wasn't struggling with sin because he was such a sinner. Paul was struggling with sin because he was such a saint."[1] We'll unpack that more later.

Clearly, history is full of examples of men in love with God, who simultaneously struggled—with sin, temptation, doubt, and depression.

Consider a few biblical examples. Job questioned God's plan for his life when he asked, "Why didn't I perish at birth?" (Job 3:11). David the adulterer was a man after God's own heart (Acts 13:22). In the midst of his struggles with sin he confessed, "My guilt has overwhelmed me like a burden too heavy to bear" (Psalms 38:4). Elijah said, "I have had enough, Lord. Take my life" (1 Kings 19:4). Those are hardly the words of preachers who had it all together. Moses killed a man (Exodus 2), Jonah despised the conversions of thousands of sinners and wanted to die (Jonah 4), Jeremiah cursed the day he was born (Jeremiah 20:14), and Peter denied even knowing Jesus—three times (Luke 22).

The Hall-of-Fame of great Christian leaders is filled with men and women who struggled. Martin Luther doubted his own salvation, Charles Spurgeon battled fits of worthlessness, John Calvin battled unbelief, C.S. Lewis endured long periods of personal doubt, Mother Teresa spoke of her personal hypocrisy and doubts about her faith, and Pope Francis has confessed to struggles with doubt. When asked by David Frost to describe his life with one word, Billy Graham said, "Failure."[2]

Let's return to our question. *Can a man love God and porn at the same time?* Unless one sets porn aside from the thousands of other struggles that godly men have battled in the midst of their spiritual walks, the historical response must be "Yes." If Peter can deny knowing Jesus weeks before the Pentecost sermon; if Elijah can run from God on the immediate heels of his greatest triumph; if David can commit adultery and have a man put to death while still leading Israel to her greatest heights; if Luther, Calvin and Mother Teresa could struggle with their faith while impacting the world with the imprint of Christ—yes, a person can love God and porn at the same time.

But let's be clear. The man who battles porn addiction while seeking a dynamic walk with God will be the model of the "double-minded man" of James 1:8. If you love God and are still mired in your addiction, prepare for countless sleepless nights, unfulfilled relationships, long periods of guilt and shame, powerlessness, and unspeakable despair and depression.

The good news for the sex addict is that while he may still love porn, that doesn't mean he has to be enslaved by it. I love chocolate filled Shipley's donuts. There was a time when I ate at least one every day. To this day, when I drive by a Shipley's, I am triggered. I remember the taste as clearly as if I had indulged minutes before. I want another donut, for the last one only satisfied for the moment. But I know eating another donut will only harm my body, in disobedience to the command about being the temple of the Holy Spirit (1 Corinthians 6:19). But knowing the Scripture doesn't remove the craving. My 267 days of donut sobriety have yet to remove my love for chocolate filled donuts. So yes, I love those donuts at the same time I love God.

If you are addicted to porn, your love for God will likely not take that away. The honest question is not *which one you will love*, but rather *which one will you serve*?

An Experiential Response

I hesitate to offer an experiential response to the big question—*Can a man love God and porn at the same time*? My theology informs me that personal experience is trumped by biblical revelation. So don't read too much into personal experience.

I can only speak for myself. While living in my addiction, the cycle introduced by sex addiction trailblazer Patrick Carnes described my experience perfectly. The four phases of the addiction cycle are: preoccupation, ritualization, compulsive sexual behavior, and despair. For the believer, that final phase—despair—is usually filled with genuine repentance and brokenness.

Again, I can only speak for myself. While living in my addiction, I read the Bible nearly every day. I maintained an active prayer list. I practiced the spiritual disciplines on a daily basis. I shared my faith with others. I was in men's groups, Bible studies, and at least three worship services per week.

In response to my addiction, I sought counseling. I was sincere about seeking help, as I spent thousands of dollars on therapy. I went to Stephen Arterburn's men's retreat. I fasted for six days, begging God to remove my destructive desires. I confessed my sin, repented of my sin, and prayed some more. I shared my struggles with my men's accountability partners, read countless books on sex addiction, and I prayed some more. I confessed my struggles—not all of them, but some of them—to my wife and my best friend, and I prayed some more. I confessed my struggles to God when alone with him on the mountain, by the lake, and on the beach. Then I prayed some more.

Still, I was addicted. I didn't want to be, but I was.

I can only speak for myself. As of this writing, I have attended about 800 12-Step meetings. I try to get to two each week, to this day. I have never been in a fellowship that is more real, genuine, and transparent than a good 12-Step meeting. Men share their greatest struggles. They share things they have never told another human being. So, as much as is possible, in these meetings, we really get to know each other. I mean really *know* each other.

And this is what I have learned. My groups are filled with God-loving, Christ-following, Bible-reading, church-attending men. By a disproportionate number, I have found Christians in 12-Step meetings. They are some of the most genuine, spiritual men in my life. We text Bible verses back and forth throughout the week. We pray for one another. We share our stories of addiction—and recovery—honestly and openly.

My experience is that men can love God and porn at the same time. I see it every week. I know these men and they know me. But again, I can only speak for myself.

A Physiological Response

One of the great benefits of attaining my Master's Degree in Addiction Recovery was the study of the physiology of sex addiction. This space does not allow for an extensive discussion on the subject, but I will hit a couple of high points.

There are several contributors to sexual addiction. To be an addict is not a decision a person makes. There are many contributing causes, such as abnormal levels of sex hormones and chemicals in the brain, such as dopamine. There are brain abnormalities, childhood abuse, and emotional trauma. Emerging data suggest a correlation between porn addiction and OCD, alcoholism, and eating disorders.

On average, a person is first exposed to porn by age 11, usually not by choice. And rarely is early exposure to porn just a one-time occurrence. This triggers a neurological response that begins a journey of no return. Neuropsychologist Dr. Tim Jennings says it like this: "Any type of repetitive behavior will create trails in our brain that are going to fire on an automatic sequence."[3]

Dr. Bob Hughes, a clinical psychologist, says his views of sex addiction have evolved as he has studied the compulsion and treated thousands of patients. He now describes sex addiction as both a sinful choice and a biological disease. He says a series of poor sexual choices turns into "an addiction which can grab onto a person and rob him of his volition."[4]

The result for many men and women is years of unsolicited bondage. That is why 62 percent of men can love God enough to be in church every Sunday, while still struggling with porn on the side. They love God with all their hearts, but are trapped in sexual bondage. The cycle is so hard to break. To whom do they go? They certainly can't stand up in most Sunday school classes and say, "Hi, my name is Larry, and I'm a sexaholic." So the struggle continues. Their repeated use of porn has literally changed the physical structure of their brains.

We know that 81 percent of sex addicts were abused as children—and zero percent of them chose that abuse. But in every case, this sets the brain on a course that isn't good.

Every C.S.A.T. (Certified Sex Addiction Therapist) will confirm that sex addiction is an intimacy disorder. Often, it is triggered in the brain by isolation. This comes in many forms. When we isolate as children, we are at risk. It was not until I got into serious recovery that I realized how my own isolation contributed to my addiction. As a young child, bones in my lower legs had not formed correctly, so I wore painful leg braces. This limited my physical activity, so I couldn't play with the other children in my neighborhood. By the age of eight, I was legally blind (20/200), which meant wearing the biggest, thickest, horn-rimmed glasses of any third grader alive. On top of that, I stuttered until I was 15—not horribly, but enough to get laughed at daily. So what did I do? I sat in the back of every class, avoided speaking at all costs, got picked last for every team at recess, and had few friends. I hated going to school.

I was alone. And I was a sitting duck for sex addiction—though I could have never seen it coming.

Are porn and sex addiction a moral issue or a physiological issue? The answer is yes. Sex addicts do not choose their addiction. But they do choose what they do about it. And unfortunately, because the road to recovery is so difficult, so long, and marked by unexpected turns, it is a road less traveled. There are cliffs to either side of the road, and the traveler can lose his sobriety with just one bad turn or choice.

Porn addiction is a physiological problem. When exposed to alcohol, nicotine, caffeine, chocolate, or porn—whether by choice or not—the journey toward addiction begins. Toss in abuse and isolation, and the surprise is not that so many are addicted to porn—but that so many are finding recovery.

So physiology and neurology give us an answer. *A man can love God and porn at the same time.*

A Theological Response

I am interested in what Patrick Carnes, Mark Laaser, Doug Weiss, and Stephen Arterburn have to say about sex addiction. I am interested in what my sponsor has to say, what my sponsees have to say, and what you have to say. But mostly, I am interested in what God has to say about porn and sex addiction. I want a biblical response to my condition. Because my theology is rooted in Scripture, it is there that I must turn. I offer a five-point theological response to addiction.

1. We are all born into sin.

We are sinners because we sin. But the opposite is also true. We sin because we are sinners. For the porn addict, the root of his problem is not his family of origin, but original sin. The psalmist declared, "I was brought forth in sin. And in sin my mother conceived me" (Psalms 51:5). Paul wrote, "In me nothing good dwells" (Romans 7:18). Whether addicts or not, we all share this in common—we were all born into sin.

2. Sin is both a condition and a choice.

That great theologian Mark Twain wrote, "Adam was but human—this explains it all. He didn't want the apple for the apple's sake. He wanted it only because it was forbidden."[5] Adam craved the "apple" for a variety of reasons. But even the most intriguing temptation didn't override his free choice. No matter the height of a person's addiction, no matter how great his temptation, every slip, relapse, or fall is the result of his personal choice. The addict must own his disease. Is it fair for the addict to ask, "Why was I the one abused as a child? Why was I the one who found his father's porn stash at age 12? Why was I the one whose parents demonstrated no affection? Why did I fall into an addiction I deplore?" Yes, all those questions are fair game. But an addict's addiction is no excuse for a single act of sexual impurity. Sin is a condition. But it is also a choice.

3. Struggle with sin never goes away.

Let's consider the struggle of Paul. His story is told in Romans 7. From the passages below, notice the intensity of his personal frustration and pain.

"I do not understand what I do. For what I want to do I do not do, but what I hate to do" (7:15).

"In me nothing good dwells" (7:18).

"I have the desire to do what is good, but I cannot carry it out" (7:18).

"I do not the good I want to do, but the evil I do not want to do—this I keep on doing. Now if I do what I do not want to do, it is no longer I who does it, but it is sin living in me that does it" (7:19-20).

"Wretched man that I am!" (7:24).

Struggle with sin never goes away. For the addict, his temptation is a reliable companion, his most enduring unwanted partner. Luther coined the Latin phrase—*simul Justus et peccator*—the simultaneously righteous and sinner. Paul was both saint and sinner at the same time. To repeat J.I. Packer, "Paul wasn't struggling with sin because he was such a sinner. Paul was struggling with sin because he was such a saint."[6]

Paul fought the temptations of sin. He found himself doing what he didn't want to do and not doing what he should. He wanted to do right, but often fell short of that goal. Paul confessed his own ignorance—"I don't understand what I do" (7:15). I count dozens of porn and sex addicts among my circle of friends. I talk to some of them every day. Most of them battle their addiction with all of their might and power. Sometimes, they fail. More often, they succeed. But always, they keep on fighting.

In his classic exposition on the Book of Romans, Donald Barnhouse wrote, "The believer in Christ is given power to overcome the outbreaks of Adamic nature, but its presence constantly contaminates his life on earth."[7] Like the porn addict, Paul struggled, but he never gave up. And it was in that struggle that he proved the strength of his faith. An addict needn't feel shame over his addiction; the real shame is when he quits trying to overcome.

4. While we may not know freedom from addiction, we can know freedom in addiction.

Jude wrote of a God "who is able to keep you from stumbling" (Jude 24). Notice he didn't promise that God would keep us from *struggling*. Many times, we ask God to take us out of the storm when his better plan is to take us *through* it. Before coming to Christ, we lived under the *penalty* of sin. Now we wrestle with the *power* of sin. There will come a time when we will be freed from the *presence* of sin.

A true Christ-follower knows the struggle of sin. Luther said, "Be a sinner and sin strongly, but more strongly have faith and rejoice in Christ."[8] The addict must not abandon his faith. Matthew Henry summarized Paul's struggle with sin: "Paul could not deliver himself; none of us can."[9] It is when we accept our condition that we find freedom.

5. What God allows today, he will use tomorrow.

Charles Stanley writes, "The scars of sin can lead us to restoration and a renewed intimacy with God."[10] John Wesley said, "Give me one hundred preachers who fear nothing but sin and desire nothing but God."[11] A truism I learned several years ago is that what God allows, he redeems. He will use my addiction—if I let him.

One of the great tragedies of the modern Church is its reluctance to address the crisis of sex addiction. I've never heard of a man who was ostracized from the church or even the pastorate because of a "proud look." Yet, "proud look" heads the list of the seven deadly sins listed in Scripture (Proverbs 6:16-19). Pope Gregory updated the list in 600 A.D. to include pride, greed, lust, envy, gluttony, wrath, and sloth. When's the last time you saw a church leader in the news because he ate too much (the sin of gluttony)?

None of this is to justify sex or porn addiction. *There is no excuse for acting out. None. Ever.*

But what God allows, he can use. I have seen broken marriages restored and wrecked lives put back together again. But first, we must seek our redemption in Christ. John Piper was right when he said, "God is most glorified in us when we are most satisfied in him."[12]

Every morning, I pray the Third Step Prayer that is familiar to many addicts. It's a great way to start any day. It is my theological response to my addiction . . .

"God, I offer myself to you, to build with me and do with me as you will. Relieve me of the bondage of self, that I may better do your will. Take away my difficulties that I may bear witness to those I would help of your power, your love, and your way of life."

A Predictive Response

What does all this mean going forward? I predict three things. First, with the explosion of technology, sex and porn addiction will only get worse—a lot worse.

Second, Christian leaders will be increasingly vulnerable, as they isolate, lack personal accountability, and know their churches view porn as a sin too great to forgive. For too many pastors, to stand up and say, "I'm struggling with porn" is the same thing as "Please toss me to the curb." Out of personal embarrassment, disgrace, and the fear of losing their jobs, too often, clergy will not seek the help they need.

Third, the church will begin to respond to the issues of sex and porn addiction in a healthy way—*slowly*. With every pastor's fall from grace, with more recovering addicts telling their stories, the Church will awaken to this issue. It is already happening, just not very quickly. But I predict that SA will become the new AA. In 20–30 years, the Church will have an adequate, redemptive, grace-focused, restorative response to the issue. At least, that is my prayer.

The answer is a resounding yes. A person can love God and porn at the same time. If I didn't believe that, I wouldn't be in recovery myself. If I didn't believe that, Beth and I wouldn't be telling our stories. Because we believe the answer is Yes! we formed this ministry and gave it the name that has kept us going through decades of struggle, addiction, and despair—*There's Still Hope.*

Signs of Trouble

Pastor, you are vulnerable. Your spiritual desire to honor God will inevitably clash with your sexual desire to soothe your pain, disappointments, and trauma. If you weren't aware of this dichotomy, you probably wouldn't have picked up this book. I don't have to try to convince you that danger lies ahead. But what I can do is give you some signs, so you can avert the danger before it hits. In working with hundreds of sex and porn addicts, many of whom are pastors, I have noticed five very specific signs of trouble.

1. You choose isolation over community.

Sexual sin always begins in secret. We act out in our head before we ever act out in our bed. And the only way to keep your sin a secret is to avoid all community. Learn this truth—loneliness and isolation are not inevitable; they are choices. Solitude is a gift from God, but isolation is a tool of the enemy.

2. You stop confessing your sins.

This is a gradual change. We go from confessing our sins (specifically) to our sin (generally). It is critical that you keep your sins before you when they come. Acknowledge them to yourself and then to God. Otherwise, small sins become huge. A stubbed toe becomes a broken leg. Tendencies become habits.

3. You no longer consider the consequences.

A really bad sign of danger is when you find yourself no longer considering the results of what you are doing. This kind of thinking only serves to lead to trouble. When tempted to act out, remember the pain this will cause, the ministry you will lose, and the people you will disappoint. Never forget that your addiction will take you further than you want to go, cost you more than you want to pay, and keep you longer than you want to stay.

4. You think the rules don't apply to you.

Carey Nieuwhof writes, "This may be the reason leaders fail more than any other. You begin to think the rules don't apply to you. So you ignore them, skirt them, rewrite them or spit in their face. Leaders who avoid accountability still eventually have to give account for their actions."[13] This is the perfect description of any leader who plays with fire.

5. You see failure as your best option.

Sometimes, we can become so despondent that we convince ourselves that this action we are considering—porn, masturbation, an affair—is a *bad option*, but it might be our *best option*. Some pastors rationalize, "Sure, I know this is wrong, but my marriage is so bad, this can't be any worse." They are so anxious to self-medicate that in the moment anything seems better than the pain they currently face.

Chapter 4
WHO CAN YOU TELL?

In an old episode of *Hill Street Blues*, police officers vainly try to cope with the increased insanity that the Christmas season visits upon both the neighborhood and the officers. One eccentric officer named Belker was a single man who played Santa Claus in a hospital ward, trying to bring comfort and cheer to suffering children. But on Christmas Eve, he is home alone, eating junk food and watching cartoons on TV. When the phone rings, he is surprised and looks hopeful. But it is the wrong number. Belker wishes the accidental caller an anonymous "Merry Christmas!"

We are all created for connection. That's why God said it was not good for man to be alone. Unfortunately, for pastors, this journey into connection often comes up empty. One study found that 70 percent of pastors don't have a single close friend.[1]

When we enter the world of sexual sin, it is especially difficult for pastors to find a trusted ear. They know that any disclosure of unacceptable behavior will be met with the harshest response. Barna researchers asked 3,000 Christians what should happen if a pastor is caught using porn. Just over 40 percent of adult Christians believe the pastor should be fired or asked to resign. However, only eight percent of the pastors agreed with termination or resignation as the appropriate response.[2]

Pastors are rightly held to a higher standard than others. Paul told Timothy that elders must be "above reproach" (1 Timothy 3:2). James warns, "Not many of you should become teachers, because you know that we who teach will be judged with greater strictness" (James 3:1).

Collin Hansen, of The Gospel Coalition, writes, "This standard presents a difficult situation for pastors in dealing with their own temptations and sin. If they try to conceal their sin, they imperil their souls. If they confess their sin, they risk losing their jobs, even if what they confess doesn't disqualify them according to Scripture. Healthy spirituality is only possible when sin can be openly confessed, but this is a tricky thing for pastors to do well."[3]

Pastors Are Loners

One of the things that drives pastors into self-preservation becomes their most daunting foe—isolation. Pastors are loners by nature. They tend to study alone, counsel alone, and stand alone. They are often not trusting of others, for they have been burned.

Writing for *Christian Ministry*, pastors David J. McFarlane and Thomas H. Yorty explain, "Pastors tend to be loners. We spend a lot of time alone in our studios, alone in our cars, alone in the chancel, alone with the needs and joys of our congregants. The spiritual journey requires some degree of silence and privacy. We function as extroverts, but at our center we tend to be introverts. Though to be alone is not necessarily to be lonely, the isolation of pastors is a bane as well as a blessing."[4]

Because they are loners, most pastors have few people with whom they can share their greatest joys, let alone their deepest sorrows. Secrecy becomes a way of life.

A Spiritual Journey

Many times throughout my 31 years as a senior pastor, the words of the psalmist became my words: "For God alone my soul waits in silence, for my hope is in him" (Psalm 62:5). Henri Nouwen said it so well. "To live a spiritual life we must first find the courage to enter into the desert of our loneliness and to change it by gentle and persistent efforts into a garden of solitude."[5]

The loneliness that is thrust upon vocational ministers does not absolve them from their responsibility of right living. We must be clear. Every sexual sin is a choice. Our pasts may be littered with isolation, trauma, and abuse. All of this may explain our behaviors, but this does not excuse our behaviors. As Arnold Dallimore observed, "When we think too lightly of sin, we think too lightly of the Savior."[6]

The walk of a pastor is one that others cannot fully grasp. The pressures are unique and the burdens heavy. It is imperative that the "man of God" work on his spiritual life above all else. Not only will this serve to preserve him from moral failure, it will equip him to find his help when he needs it the most.

A Healthy Response

For the moment, let's set aside the discussion of a man's spiritual journey and the reasons for his struggle. Let's get practical. A wise minister will set in place an infrastructure of accountability and connection before the temptations to fall ever present themselves. Why? Not just because this is the wise thing to do, but because it is the healthy thing to do.

According to research from UCLA, talking can diminish the response of your brain's amygdala, which initiates the fight or flight response when you're feeling intense emotions like fear, anxiety, or aggression.[7]

In general, strong relationships, having someone to talk to, is linked to longer life. In contrast, social isolation and loneliness are linked to depression, poorer health outcomes, and risk of premature death.[8] It is clear that the healthy thing for every pastor to do is to be intentional about human connection.

Some Good Ideas

Let's get practical. I suggest you read an article by Pastor Joshua Reich, "Why Most Pastors Are Nice People but Don't Make Good Friends."[9] Reich suggests five specific steps be taken by every pastor: (a) have friends who don't attend your church, (b) have a no-church talk zone, (c) take a day off, (d) get in a small group, and (e) get a hobby.

I will add a few suggestions to that list. Build friendships with pastors from other churches. Establish long-distance relationships. Work on your relationships at home. And engage in nonproductive relationships. By this, I mean, join a car club, take dance lessons (unless you're Baptist), get into a civic club. In each of these places, you will establish casual friendships with men to whom you may never be particularly close. And that's okay; it provides an emotional and relational outlet, which is healthy.

The Fruit of Confessing Sin

Before tackling the question of pastoral confession, let's discuss the value of anyone confessing any sin. We sometimes hear from clients, "If all my sins are forgiven in Christ, why do I need to confess my sins to God?" And the natural outcome of not confessing sins to God would be to not confess our struggles to man, either. The result would be that addicts would just retreat to the crevices of their own minds and live with unresolved shame.

Let's unpack this issue. There are several reasons a Christ-follower is wise to tell someone about his sin, struggles, and addictions. All of this applies to the pastor.

1. Confession maintains the fellowship.

While our relationship with God was established when we were born again, our fellowship with him can ebb and flow, depending on our obedience. Through union with Christ by faith, we stand justified in his righteousness, and there is nothing we can do to lose that relationship. Our communion with God, on the other hand, is dependent on both obedience and how we deal with disobedience.

Human relationships function in a similar manner. A faithful response to confess our sins to other believers fuels recovery and hope. Confession clears the way for close communion with other Christ-followers. Confession is both vertical (with God) and horizontal (with other people).

2. Confession fosters fear.

Pastor and author J. Garrett Kell writes, "Receiving forgiveness cultivates proper fear."[10] By that he seems to mean that telling another person our struggle creates a fresh layer of accountability. When you as a pastor confess your struggle to another human being, the fear of losing your sobriety becomes a powerful tool.

My story of addiction and recovery is not something I hide. I estimate that I have shared my story with at least 200 different men in "secular" 12-Step groups, about 75 pastors, and an audience of several thousand through speaking engagements, podcast interviews, books, articles, etc. The thought of letting these people down isn't my best motivation to stay sober, but it's a pretty good one.

3. Confession stirs thankfulness.

The connection between sexual purity and gratitude is clear: "Sexual immorality and all impurity or covetousness must not even be named among you, as is proper among saints. Let there be no filthiness nor foolish talk nor crude joking, which are out of place, but instead let there by thanksgiving" (Ephesians 5:3-4).

Kell writes, "A grumbling heart feels justified in sinful escapes, but a thankful one finds contentment in whatever God provides."[11] There is nothing quite like telling another brother our pain and sin and receiving a kind response. As a pastor, this is especially true.

How to Find Someone to Talk To

If you're like most pastors, you may assume that you have no one to talk to, especially if you live far from your family. But you need someone to talk to, particularly in times of crisis. Here are a few suggested ways to find that person.

1. Make a list of social connections.

This is a good place to start. Include people you know from a variety of situations like family members, friends, social media contacts, and men from civic groups or other community organizations. Try to narrow your list to those who are emotionally intelligent, but also emotionally skilled. Such people are more empathetic.

Invite some of these men to coffee or lunch. Begin to share your heart with them, not just the details of your ministry. This is a lifelong process. By cultivating these friendships over the passage of years, you will have the right contacts when you really need them.

2. Join a support group.

There are more support groups than you can imagine. A good place to start, for those pastors who struggle with sexual issues, is my pastors' Freedom Group, which is a gathering of pastors who meet each week online. Whether you join an online group or an in-person group, this option can provide you with a network of people who can relate to what you are experiencing.

3. Work with a therapist.

Whether you need to discuss a mental health issue, how to manage stress, or a personal sexual integrity issue, a good therapist is a great place to start. Dr. Mike MacKenzie writes, "A pastor or missionary can hire a Christian counselor, spiritual mentor, or coach. Not only does this relationship serve the purpose of having a confessor but has the additional benefit of helping in additional growth or insight."[12] I always encourage clients to pursue therapy with a C.S.A.T. (Certified Sex Addiction Therapist). Such counselors are trained to help you develop healthier coping mechanisms and can direct you into a network of support.

4. Go to another church when possible.

You will find it healthy to connect with various worship expressions and traditions. Throughout my pastoral ministry, I found it helpful to connect with pastors from various denominations. I tried to have lunch with a different pastor each month. Getting outside your own church and connecting with other worship environments will lead to more positive social interactions.[13]

Why We Don't Want to Tell

While at the height of my pastoral ministry, my therapist told me, "You really need to share your story with someone."

My response: "You've got to be kidding me!"

Leading churches over a span of three decades taught me to say nothing of my personal struggles. My mantra was, "Anything I say can be used against me." And it was true.

There are three specific reasons pastors are reticent to tell their stories.

1. Fear of criticism

Pastors are among society's most criticized lot to start with. When we fall, instead of letting down our guards, we feel that we must be prepared to defend or articulate the reason for a decision or direction. We dodge and minimize, not because we want to hide, but because we fear the fall-out of criticism.

2. Pain of betrayal

I don't know of a minister with more than ten minutes of experience who has not been betrayed. We tell the wrong person. We share too much of our story. Our timing is off. Whatever the reasons, we have handed a club to our "friend," with which they can beat us if they so choose. I can't count the number of people to whom I told my story, only to have them betray my confidence. After just one such instance, most of us respond with total withdrawal.

3. Feeling of being overwhelmed

Ministry is overwhelming if all goes perfectly, which, of course, it never does. Add to that the emotionally draining experience of telling someone your darkest secrets and you will have a formula for an emotional breakdown. Just the mere thought of being known is overwhelming. Knowing that you have just told another person enough information to bury you may be necessary. But it is also exhausting.

How to Know It Went Well

Pastor, someone needs to know your story. That is non-negotiable. But how do you know it went well? What is the validation that God was really involved in this process? While we can't control outcome, we can look at that outcome, and generally see great blessings that resulted from this simple act of obedience. Here are a few examples.

1. You are liberated from the falsehood of perfection.

Despite what your church may think, you don't have an inside track to God. You are just as vulnerable as anyone else. I might argue you are actually more vulnerable. But when we share our struggles (not necessarily the details), we find freedom. It's what I call "walking with a limp." There is just something about that limp that makes a pastor more equipped to lead.

2. You show others how it's done.

You will know you "did it right" when other men come to you and say, "Pastor, I never thought I could tell another human soul about my personal problem. But when you told us about your struggles, I felt the strength to step up." The fact is, we reproduce who we are, not what we say. Demonstrating a confessional life will only help others to do the same.

3. You create safe space.

I have heard more than a few pastors brag that their church has created a class or group for men and women mired in addiction. My response is, "That is what the church was created for in the first place. We shouldn't need a subgroup to make that happen." By letting others into your struggle, you will create the environment for which the world has been yearning.

4. You will allow the church to minister to you.

The wall that separates clergy from laity is manmade. God never intended for the church to be divided in this way. We are all called to minister within and to the body of Christ. I can't think of a better example of how the body of Christ is supposed to work than when a pastor confesses a personal sin and the congregation responds with grace and redemption.

Chapter 5
ARE YOU DISQUALIFIED FROM MINISTRY?

No one is really qualified for ministry.

There. I said it. Now, let me explain. If you read through the 18 biblical qualifications for a pastor/elder, listed below, and you are truly honest, you will have to admit that no one really scores a "100" on this scorecard. But rarely is a pastor dismissed because his child is out of control (1 Timothy 3:4-5). If we fired every minister who exhibited arrogance (Titus 1:7), there would be a lot of empty pulpits this Sunday. Have you ever known a really effective pastor who didn't occasionally fall short in these areas: hospitality (Titus 1:8), self-control (1 Timothy 3:2), and the full respect of his community (1 Timothy 3:7)?

No one is really qualified for ministry.

I remember my college professor, Dr. Paul Brooks Leath, saying often, "There is no connection between the size of a man's ministry and his personal walk with God." The good news is that there has never been a pastor who was so upright that he could not fall, nor a man so low that he could not be used by God. Remember, each of us is a sinner. We all have committed adultery in our hearts. We all have indulged in lust. We all have lost control of our thoughts, our tongues, and our hearts.

No one is really qualified for ministry.

I'm sure you have heard this many times, but it certainly bears repeating. God does not call the qualified; he qualifies the called. This is not to give any pastor a pass when he commits gross sexual sin. Nor is it to say sexual addictions should not result in a man's removal from office. My point is simply that there is none who does not sin. And when we apply the strict standards of 1 Timothy and Titus, we really have to come to one conclusion.

No one is really qualified for ministry.

Biblical Qualifications

It is not my purpose to dig into the specifics of what might disqualify a person from ministry. Volumes have been written on the subject. Various denominations and faith traditions will land at different places in this arena. What may be disqualifying for one church might not be for another. That said, it is always a good reminder to read over some of the biblical declarations of the qualifications for a person serving as a pastor (or elder). I'll let the Scripture speak for itself.

- A pastor is to be above reproach (I Timothy 3:2, Titus 1:6).
- A pastor must be devoted to his wife (1 Timothy 3:2, Titus 1:6).
- A pastor's children must not be unruly (1 Timothy 3:4-5, Titus 1:6).
- A pastor is to be a faithful steward (Titus 1:7).
- A pastor must be humble and not arrogant (Titus 1:7).
- A pastor must be gentle, not quick-tempered (1 Timothy 3:3, Titus 1:7).
- A pastor must be sober, not a drunkard (1 Timothy 3:3, Titus 1:7).
- A pastor must be peaceful, not violent (1 Timothy 3:3, Titus 1:7).
- A pastor must have financial integrity, not greedy of gain (1 Timothy 3:3, Titus 1:7, I Peter 5:3).
- A pastor must be hospitable (1 Timothy 3:2, Titus 1:8).
- A pastor must be a lover of what is good (Titus 1:8).
- A pastor must be self-controlled (1 Timothy 3:2, Titus 1:8).
- A pastor must be upright (Titus 1:8).
- A pastor must be holy (Titus 1:8).

- A pastor must be able to teach (1 Timothy 3:2, Titus 1:9).
- A pastor must be spiritually mature (1 Timothy 3:6).
- A pastor must be respectable (1 Timothy 3:7).
- A pastor must be an example to the church (1 Peter 5:3).

Simple Overview

While we will inevitably disagree on the specifics of what qualifies and disqualifies a man for ministry, I think we can agree on three basic tenets. These seem so self-evident that they will only be given brief consideration.

1. Some sins disqualify a person from public ministry.

Let's state the absurd. If a pastor shoots a deacon with a pistol, he has disqualified himself from ministry (all obvious jokes aside). If a pastor is living with a woman other than his wife, he can no longer serve. If he is unrepentant of obvious sins such as public drunkenness, he must step aside. All of us can agree on these examples. John MacArthur writes, "We must not lower our standards in order to accommodate a leader's sin."[1] A study among church leaders found that a significant majority of U.S. protestant pastors share the opinion that "any person who has committed sexual abuse is permanently disqualified from holding the office of pastor.[2]

2. Some sins absolutely do not disqualify a pastor.

A church is unlikely to fire her pastor because he missed his morning devotions one day. The fact that he has abused his temple of the Holy Spirit with too many Twinkies will probably not land him in serious jeopardy. When the pastor commits other sins such as driving over the speed limit, cutting in line at the grocery store, or rooting for the wrong football team, the church will likely look the other way.

Of course, we all have been disappointed in something our pastor has said or done. No pastor will please everyone all the time. While this book it written for pastors who are broken, our hope is that the church will find truth and application in these pages, as well. So if you are a non-staff church member, hear this—pray for your pastor! Pastor and writer Jeramie Rinne, who serves the Evangelical Community Church in Abu Dhabi, United Arab Emirates, writes, "Pastors face the regular temptation to fear people instead of God. They wrestle with their own sinful tendencies to please others at the expense of biblical principles. Pray that your pastor would love God, and you, so much that he would be willing to disappoint you for God's glory."[3] Let me suggest several ways in which you can pray for your pastor, when you are tempted to criticize him.

    a. Pray that your pastor would fear God and not man.
    b. Pray that your pastor would have great confidence in God's Word and the Gospel.
    c. Pray that your pastor would love his family well.
    d. Pray that your pastor would grow in godliness.
    e. Pray that your pastor would hate sin and love righteousness.
    f. Pray that your pastor would love church members.
    g. Pray that your pastor would love his community.
    h. Pray that your pastor would have great wisdom.
    i. Pray that your pastor would find rest.

3. Most sins fall somewhere in the middle.

What do you do with the pastor whom you discovered lied on his resume when you hired him 20 years ago? What about the man who has lust in his heart (which meets Jesus' definition of adultery)? What if your pastor is often found at business lunches with just his female assistant? Is a trip to the casino okay? What about drinking? If so, how much? And if the pastor has committed adultery with a woman and repented of it, then walked in freedom for 30 years, should he be released from the church upon this discovery? What if it's been just five years? The "What ifs" go on endlessly. The point is, the line which a pastor crosses that is beyond repair is drawn in sand. Reasonable minds can disagree. John Piper is right: "I don't think this is the kind of issue where the church as a whole will ever have agreement."[4]

Factors that Determine the Severity of the Situation

Let's be clear. All sexual sin is devastating. To not commit adultery is a command, not a suggestion. Lustful thoughts, according to the Savior, don't lead to adultery—they are adultery. And with God, there are no shades of sin. Sin is sin and sexual sin is sexual sin.

Having established that, we must understand that while all sin is sin, the effects of sin will vary. For example, there's never been a wife who would view her husband's double take when an attractive woman walked into his peripheral vision on the same level as having sexual relations with the next door neighbor.

Our purpose here is not to define which sexual sins constitute removal of a pastor from his vocational office. Rather, we simply want to present the case for thoughtful reflection before responding to the sexual misconduct of a pastor. The following three considerations may help to frame that discussion.

1. Content: What was he viewing, exactly?

We established in the first chapter that a great majority of evangelical men (62 percent) struggle with porn, including 37 percent of pastors. What we have not offered is a definition of pornography. Nor will we do so here. You see, while there are certain images that certainly qualify as "porn" by nearly all standards, there are other images that can be placed in one man's "inner circle" (breaking his sobriety), but another's "middle circle" (dangerous, but not breaching sobriety).

When judging the depth of your pastor's behaviors and porn viewing, identify the type of porn he has been viewing. It does matter.

    a. Printed adult pornography
    b. Online adult pornography
    c. Swimsuit catalogues
    d. Sports Illustrated Swimsuit Edition
    e. Lingerie ads
    f. Child pornography
    g. Violent pornography

h. Same-sex pornography

2. Frequency: How often did the pastor view pornography?

It is estimated that 99 percent of all men (including Christians) have viewed pornography. Most churches would not toss their pastor to the curb if they found out that at some point in his life, he has used porn. Frequency matters. But let's be clear. If the church is to restore her pastor to his office, no porn is acceptable from this day forward. Having established that, church leadership will want to know the depth of the problem. One way to do that is to assess the frequency of the pastor's porn use.

a. Once a year?
b. Once a month?
c. Once a week?
d. Once a day?

3. Physicality: Did it involve a live person?

Calvary Chapel Pastor Ed Taylor speaks for many when he says succinctly, "It should come as no surprise that adultery is an immediate disqualification from ministry."[5] That begs the question, "What is adultery?" Given Jesus' definition of adultery, should we fire every pastor the second he thinks of a woman with lust in his heart? Is porn use a form of adultery? (I would offer an emphatic Yes!) But whether a man commits lust with pornography or a physical sexual act does matter. It certainly matters to the man's wife, and therefore should matter to his church, as well.

Assessing a Man's True Recovery

One pastor, living in two adulterous relationships, shared, "This was the insanity: I no sooner finished the sexual act and immediately broke into tears, devastated by what I had done, but I only returned again and again to the same sinful relationship."[6]

Sadly, this story has been repeated thousands of times—among pastors alone. If that is you, pastor, the only thing that matters now is what you do next. If you are a church leader, assessing the future of a fallen pastor, I suggest you judge him, not only by what he did wrong, but by what he may be doing right—now. Three factors indicate the sincerity and success of a pastor's progress.

1. Trajectory

Recovery is about direction, not destination. We never arrive. Sexual temptation is mitigated, not eliminated. The important thing is the trajectory of a man's recovery. Is he taking positive steps in the right direction? Is he progressing through the 12 Steps? Or is he regressing in his recovery work? If the pastor is on the right pathway, he will gladly open the door for church leaders to communicate with someone who is personally involved in his recovery efforts. He will offer to do periodic clinical disclosures and polygraphs for his wife and church. He will want others to look closely into his personal decisions and lifestyle choices.

The American Addiction Centers offer good counsel on the progress one can expect to make in his recovery. "The best attitude to keep in recovery is a beginner's mind. The individual should always be open to having his current beliefs and opinions challenged."[7] If the pastor in recovery does this, he will remain on a trajectory of success.

2. Honesty

Those people who are trying to rebuild their lives after an addiction need to pay particular attention to honesty. They need to not only be truthful with other people, but more importantly with themselves. Failure to establish honesty as a personal quality may mean that the individual will be more at risk of relapse. It could also mean that they live a life that is not fulfilling. The staff of the Cleveland Alcoholics Anonymous district writes, "Honesty is what finally leads people into recovery, and it is the one thing that keeps them there."[8] Several questions help to measure a pastor's honesty in his efforts toward recovery.

Has the pastor come clean? Is he willing to take a polygraph? Is he willing to be accountable to another man, perhaps someone assigned by the church? Or does he only confess to those things for which he has already been caught? Scotty Smith, writing for the Gospel Coalition, says, "A group of godly elders must be involved in the situation, in order to walk beside the pastor over a period of time."[9]

3. Recovery efforts

At the time of the discovery, was the pastor in recovery? If so, for how long? What efforts has he made to become whole? Has he demonstrated a commitment to those things that feed recovery—therapy, meetings, etc.?

Five Considerations

The basic discussion of whether the pastor has disqualified himself from ministry might best be framed within the context of a few basic concepts. Perhaps the following principles will serve you well in deciding—if you are the pastor—whether you are qualified for public ministry, now or in the future. Pastor Garrett Kell warns against falling into either ditch—not taking sin seriously enough and not taking grace seriously enough.[10] These concepts might serve the church as a whole.

1. Be willing to make the tough decisions.

When God inspired 1 Timothy 3 and Titus 1, he knew this would present great stress points for the modern church. Given the requirement that a pastor's children not be unruly (just one example), the case could be made that none of us is qualified to serve. The truth is, most of us—and most of our churches—tend to run to one end of the spectrum or the other. Some enforce the rules of these two biblical passages with such rigidity that any fallen pastor is doomed to stay down. Others claim to be more "grace oriented." But this may really be a way to avoid tough choices and confrontation. As a pastor, you need to make the tough decision, which might mean stepping away, even when not forced to do so. And the church may need to terminate her pastor, even if true remorse and repentance are present. Pastor Joe McKeever writes, "You are unqualified if you are unwilling to pay the price to keep your heart pure, your example strong, and your reputation spotless."[11]

2. Separate forgiveness from restoration.

There is a difference between being forgiven and being trusted. Any betrayed spouse can attest to that truth. Forgiveness is based on the blood of Jesus Christ and can be granted and received instantaneously upon genuine repentance. But regaining trust can take years, if it is even possible at all. If you as a pastor have betrayed your church by means of infidelity (that includes porn use), don't confuse forgiveness with restoration. Forgiveness has no time boundary to it. It is never too soon to forgive or be forgiven. But restoration takes time, a specific plan, and hard work.

Let's look at the difference between forgiveness and restoration. First, a few thoughts about forgiveness, as suggested by Rose Sweet, with Focus on the Family.[12]

a. Forgiveness is not letting the offender off the hook.
b. Forgiveness is returning to God the right to take care of justice.
c. Forgiveness is not letting the offense recur again and again.
d. Forgiveness does not mean we have to revert to being the victim.
e. Forgiveness is not the same as reconciling.
f. Forgiveness is a process, not an event.
g. We have to forgive every time.
h. Forgiving does not mean denying reality or ignoring repeated offenses.
i. Forgiveness is not based on others' actions, but on our attitude.
j. If they don't repent, we still have to forgive.
k. We don't always have to tell them we have forgiven them.
l. Withholding forgiveness is a refusal to let go of perceived power.
m. We might have to forgive more than what we see on the surface.
n. We often offer a false forgiveness before we are ready.

o. Forgiveness does not mean forgetting.
p. Forgiveness is a decision.

Restoration is a different matter. No one disputes that there is a line which a pastor cannot cross without losing his ministry, though the exact placement of this line is debatable. So what does it mean to receive restoration? Let's consider several biblical accounts that go to the depth of the meaning of true restoration.

    a. God's Law. The concept of restoration can be traced to Levitical Law. We read this promise for those in need of healing: "If you listen carefully to the Lord your God and do what is right in his eyes, if you pay attention to his commands and keep all his decrees, I will not bring on you any of the diseases I brought on the Egyptians, for I am the Lord, who heals you" (Exodus 15:26).

    b. The story of Daniel. In the story of Daniel and his three friends, we find four men devoted to their God in the face of great temptation to defile themselves. Herein we discover the theme of restoration. "Daniel resolved not to defile himself with the royal food and wine, and he asked the chief official for permission not to defile himself in this way" (Daniel 1:8). The Hebrew word for defile, *ga'al*, means to pollute, stain, or desecrate. It was through personal devotion and sacrifice that these four men were restored to the fullest health and blessing.

    c. The New Covenant. In Jeremiah 31:31-34, God describes the new covenant made with God's beloved people. In this covenant language, one can see God's plan to restore his people to his original intention. Lillian Tryon writes, "God's purpose is to restore man's right standing with him by forgiving wickedness and remembering sins no more."[13]

3. Don't quickly dismiss the damage to the church.

The damage that a pastor's sex addiction brings upon his church is hard to overstate. I like to use the analogy of a dartboard. Think of each act of betrayal as another dart thrown into the dartboard. When you have finally quit throwing darts, you can be forgiven. For our purposes here, think of forgiveness as removing those darts from the board. They are now gone. But what remain are the marks of each dart. Likewise, your sexual sin has left a mark on your church. Never forget that. Yes, you can be forgiven. And perhaps you can be restored to a position in that church. But never return void of a true empathetic understanding of the pain you have caused. Tim Challies writes, "The fall of another pastor means the agony of another church, as yet another community of Christians grapples with the fallout of their pastor's great sin."[14]

4. Seek discipline and real change.

It is not enough to accept church discipline. If you are sincere, you will actually want it. Freely pursue any kind of restitution and amends that church leaders deem appropriate. Then engage a lifetime of recovery. Go to meetings. Seek therapy. Eliminate old habits as you establish new ones. Regardless of how your church (or wife) responds, do the hard work. It took years to get into this ditch; the road out is not short. Let your serenity and integrity do your preaching now. At the dawn of the Reformation, Martin Luther preached a sermon about the righteousness of Christ. He called it an alien righteousness because it doesn't naturally belong to Christians. It is Christ's righteousness. It belongs to him. Grace means this righteousness can be ours, through faith in Christ alone. Luther said, "All that he has becomes ours and he himself becomes ours."[15] Through faith, Christ gives us himself. And with himself, he gives us the power to defeat sin in our lives.

5. Re-enter carefully.

If you are to re-enter public ministry, the timing will follow one of three patterns: (a) too soon, (b) too late, (c) just right. The only one that's bad is "too soon." Err on the side of moving slowly. We all know of well-known preachers and evangelists who fell to sexual sin, then got back up and re-entered ministry—too soon. The results can be horrendous. How long does it take to rebuild your life to the point of returning to the pulpit or some other public ministry? That's hard to say. As for me, while I considered myself permanently disqualified from normal pastoral ministry, I also thought it wise to delay the start of our ministry, There's Still Hope, until my fifth year of recovery. Be careful. Go slow. Don't rush it. The church will still be there when you are ready. The story Ray Stedman told of a fellow pastor who fell into sexual sin years ago still resonates today. "Somewhere along the line he fell into temptation; he fell into adultery, and this morning he is disqualified. I am praying, because I love him, that it will only be a temporary disqualification. God can restore him."[16]

Chapter 6
FOUR STEPS TO FREEDOM

Broken vessels can be made whole again. In the world of addiction, it's called "freedom." We all long to be free. Even the addict who spends thousands of dollars and willingly forsakes his family, all for the sake of pleasure, wants freedom. No one wants to remain a slave to his cravings. The desire for freedom is not in question for any of us.

What is in question is the way out of the darkness. What rules must be followed? What principles hold consistently for all successful recovery? What are the specific steps one must follow? And is there a biblical example of these steps?

Let's unpack each of these questions.

Five Rules of Recovery

There are some basic principles that will set up anyone for success. These are rules that cannot be broken if one hopes to find lasting recovery. While volumes have been written on the various techniques and principles of addiction recovery, these five rules are inconvertible for anyone who wants to be well. I've seen hundreds of men and women find recovery; every one of them followed these rules, whether they realized it or not.

Rule 1: Change your life.

The most important rule of recovery is that a person does not achieve recovery by simply stopping a behavior. As you will hear in recovery meetings, "Sober is not well." Recovery involves creating a new life in which it is easier to not use. When individuals do not change their lives, then all the factors that contributed to their addiction will eventually return.

The mistake many of us make is to believe that we can change our habit without changing ourselves. We want our old lives minus the behavior. But what we must understand is that the behavior was simply the predictable result of something else in our lives.

Rule 2: Be completely honest.

Addiction requires lying. Addicts lie about everything: where they got their drug of choice, how long they've been acting out, and the consequences. Until a person gets honest, he does not get well.

How honest should a person in recovery be? The concept of the recovery circle is helpful here. Within that circle the client writes the names of those who need to hear truth from him: family, counselors, self-help groups, and sponsors. This circle might be enlarged with time.[1]

Rule 3: Ask for help.

Most people seek to find recovery on their own, initially. They want to prove they have control over their addiction and they are not as unhealthy as people think. This is especially true for pastors, who, after all, have a unique relationship with God—so they think. Joining a self-help group has been proven to significantly increase the chances of long-term sobriety. The combination of addiction therapy and self-help groups is the most effective plan. This is confirmed by a three-year study of alcoholics in recovery groups.[2]

Twelve-Step groups have been found to bring special benefits to those in need. Studies on the benefits of 12-Step work find the following results of group work: (a) feeling of not being alone, (b) learning from others, (c) learning effective coping skills, (d) being a safe place to connect without judgment.[3] This is true for substance addictions, but the implications seem to hold consistent for behavioral addictions as well.

Rule 4: Practice self-care.

People turn to their addictions in search of escape, relaxation, and reward. These benefits of addiction must be acknowledged and reversed. The danger is that the addict often sees the need to punish himself by avoiding all forms of self-pleasure.

Self-care is often the most overlooked aspect of recovery. Without it, individuals can go to meetings, work a program, have a sponsor, do Step work, and still relapse. Researchers confirm that self-care is difficult because recovering individuals tend to be hard on themselves.[4]

It is critical to understand the difference between selfishness and self-care. Selfishness is taking more than a person needs. Self-care is taking as much as one needs. Clinical experience has shown that addicted people typically take less than they need, and, as a result, become exhausted or resentful.[5] They then return to their addiction eventually.

Rule 5: Don't bend the rules.

We must be reminded that what works, works. There is a tendency to bend the rules as we claim more recovery ground. People quit going to meetings, working the Steps, and doing recovery activities. Dr. Melemis writes, "Broadly speaking, once clients have been in recovery for a while, they can be divided into non-users and denied users. Non-users say that using was fun but acknowledge that it has not been fun lately. They want to start the next chapter in their life."[6]

Each of us must determine honestly whether we are a non-user or denied user. A denied user is in chronic mental relapse and is at high-risk of full relapse. Clinical experience has shown that everyone in early recovery is a denied user. The goal is to help individuals to move from denied users to non-users.

What Are the Steps To Recovery?

Recovery is both a gift and a reward. It is a gift from God, for without him, we cannot find sobriety. And it is a reward, because without us, God will not grant sobriety. Without him, we can't; without us, God won't.

But how do we break the cycle of addiction, exactly? Speaking in generalities, we must rely on God as our Higher Power. We need the structure and tested paradigm provided by the 12 Steps. Rarely does a person find sobriety apart from personal therapy. It is best to seek the services of a C.S.A.T. when possible. But here, let's identify the four key steps to successful recovery.

1. Desperation

The first step to freedom is absolute desperation. We cannot win in life—let alone in recovery—apart from desperation. Jon Bloom, author and cofounder of Desiring God, writes that "the lack of a sense of desperation for God is deadly."[7] Indeed, there are many things we can accomplish with half-hearted efforts. Recovery is not one of them.

Author Ana Menez addresses the connection of desperation to those mired in the depths of addiction. "Once you hit rock bottom, you'll find that God is there, doing something great. You will discover God in moments of desperation. Desperation is a craving, a longing. It is a thirst and an ache for an urgent need."[8] It is that urgent need that drives us to desperation. And it is in that desperation that we find hope.

2. Surrender

Living in one's addiction is a matter of control. Addicts want to control their circumstances, moods, pleasures, and other people. But they cannot control themselves. It is only when we recognize that we have a problem that we cannot solve that we are ready for recovery. Only then are we likely to turn to God.

Dwight L. Moody said, "Let God have your life; he can do more with it than you can." Only through surrender can we make the right choices.[9] A.W. Tozer wrote, "The man or woman who is wholly surrendered to Christ can't make a wrong choice—any choice will be the right one."[10] Any successful road to recovery begins with surrender. Every day, I tell myself, "I'm not saying I'll never act out again. But I am saying it won't happen today." Then I pray the Third Step prayer of surrender.

Finding sobriety is not about trying harder. Telling an addict to try harder only tightens the noose of bondage. When we tell men to just pray harder, try harder, and love Jesus more, it is like telling a crippled man to try harder to walk. We add shame to guilt. The problem is not lack of effort, but surrender. The Bible says, "The Spirit (not our own human effort) enables us to deny the flesh and resist temptation" (Romans 8:14). With surrender, a new pattern develops (Titus 2:11-12).

3. Disclosure

This is the one I fought the hardest. Early in recovery, I was okay with surrender to God. I embraced 12-Step work. But disclosure is where I drew the line. I wasn't ready to tell my story—at least not to my wife. But Mark Laaser is right when he says, "Silence is the greatest enemy of sexual health."[11]

There are three levels of disclosure. The first level is partial disclosure. With that the addict tells his or her spouse what he or she has to tell them. The addict has been caught. It's time to come clean. But because the addict is not coming clean of his or her own will, there is natural resistance. So the addict tells the spouse a little more than the spouse already knows, thinking, "This will satisfy her." Partial disclosure is the same thing as gradual disclosure—telling the wounded partner a little of one's story at a time. And there has never been a wounded spouse who preferred it this way. It's torturous. But it's what addicts do. We are liars. We tell only what we have to. Every addict starts at this level of disclosure.

The second level of disclosure is a full, non-clinical disclosure. This is a written disclosure in which the addict reads his story to his wife in the presence of a counselor. He gets the whole story out. And then his spouse has the opportunity to respond. This is normally done in one, long counseling session.

The third level of disclosure is a full clinical disclosure. This is best done as part of a three-day intensive with a trained C.S.A.T. The addict reads his story to his wife, in the presence of the therapist. Then she responds with a series of questions. This is followed by a full polygraph examination. The purpose of the polygraph is to determine whether the addict has been completely forthcoming.

I am a huge proponent of a full, clinical disclosure for three reasons. First, it finally paints the whole picture for the wounded spouse. Wives want honesty above all else. They need to know what they are dealing with in their husband's addiction. It is the fear of the unknown that haunts them the most. Second, it gives the marriage a reset. From that moment forward, the past is left in the past. Further questions about the addict's past will no longer be entertained. This gives the addict an indescribable feeling of hope and restoration. And third, a full disclosure reprograms the addict's mind toward honesty.

I resisted doing a full, clinical disclosure myself. But Beth insisted on it. Eventually, I agreed, and what resulted was the first absolute honest expression of my hurts, habits, and hang-ups (Celebrate Recovery language) she had ever heard from me. I have done three follow-up one-day clinical disclosures since—each with a fresh polygraph exam. (I have passed each polygraph exam.) I don't do this because Beth asks me to, but because I want to. I want her to experience the peace of mind that comes from knowing I am sober, free, and honest—a peace of mind I robbed from her for so many years.

Debra Laaser, co-leader of *Faithful and True Ministries*, recommends a full disclosure up front, early in recovery. "Knowing the whole truth is foundational to building a new life together, because the new structure must be built on honesty and openness."[12]

To couples who aren't sure they want to do a full, clinical disclosure (with polygraph), I say, "Why not?" If the addict is truly clean, and if he or she has truly told all of his or her story, that addict should want his or her spouse to know it as close to 100 percent as possible. If you are the wounded spouse, by accepting anything less than a polygraph, you are assuming your spouse—who has lied to you for years—is suddenly going to share with you his deepest secrets and darkest moments. And you will always have at least a hint of a doubt.

In fact, we believe in the full disclosure with polygraph so strongly that *There's Still Hope* grants scholarships. We will fund $100 of your first polygraph, if done within the context of a three-day intensive with a trained C.S.A.T. counselor.

4. Community

Recovery is a team sport. I have never met a person who found sobriety in isolation. Michael Leahy, founder of Brave-

Hearts addiction ministry, says that only one in 10,000 finds successful recovery in isolation. If fact, it is that isolation that actually drives a man into addiction in the first place. The problem cannot be the cure. For a man to try to find sobriety on his own would be as suicidal as washing down poison with more poison. The AA "Big Book" says, "The feeling of having shared in a common peril is one element in the powerful cement which binds us."[13]

Jesus set the example for healthy growth and boundaries. He was committed to community. He spent three years with 12 men, and even more time with three of the 12. But notice, though he called men to a *personal* relationship with him, he never called them to a *private* relationship with him.

The Book of James gives great insight to the necessity of community. James said, "Confess your sins one to another, that you may be healed" (James 5:16). That is stunning. James did not say, "Confess your sins *to God*." He said to confess your sins to *"one another."* The purpose of confession in a small group, James said, is healing. And that is the goal of every addict—healing. Apart from community there is no healing.

A great place to start is by joining a 12-Step group. Dr. Doug Weiss, author of *The Final Freedom: Pioneering Sexual Addiction Recovery*, suggests recovery must be tailored to the individual addict. But, he is an advocate for, "in most cases, a personal accountability partner and weekly group meetings." He writes, "I have never met anyone who has experienced sexual addiction recovery alone."[14]

A Biblical Model

An amazing miracle is recorded in John 5. You are probably familiar with the story of the paralytic, so I won't go into great depth here, other than to dig into the four steps of recovery, as seen in the paralytic's life. The setting is the pool at Bethesda, near Jerusalem, where "a great number of disabled people used to lie—the blind, the lame, the paralyzed" (John 5:3). Among the disabled was the key figure in the story, who had been paralyzed for 38 years. Jesus entered the picture, and the four steps of recovery are unpacked.

Step 1—Desperate

Until a man becomes desperate he does not get well. We pick up the story in verse 6. "When Jesus saw him lying there and learned that he had been in this condition for a long time, he asked him, 'Do you want to get well?'"

Jesus saw the crowd, but he focused on the individual. That's what Jesus does. Then he asked an odd question of a man who was there for the specific reason of getting well. (Tradition had it that the first person into the pool after the water stirred would be healed.) "Do you want to get well?" Notice the man's response.

"Sir, I have no one to help me into the pool when the water is stirred. While I am trying to get in, someone else goes down ahead of me" (John 5:7).

The man obviously wanted to become well; otherwise, he wouldn't have had his friends carry him to the water, then struggle to get into that water against all odds. Jesus didn't ask the man if he wanted to be well because he lacked that information, but because the man needed to confess his need, and the witnesses who were there needed to hear it. Jesus met the man at the point of his desperation. Some speculate that this was precisely the reason Jesus singled this man out from among the masses—he knew the desperation of his heart.

Likewise, any person who is mired in the entrapment of sexual impurity will remain mired until desperation kicks in. This is why very few go all in until they hit bottom. Until they bottom out, they are not quite ready to embrace whatever is needed to become well.

Step 2—Surrender

The story continues. "Then Jesus said to him, 'Get up! Pick up your mat and walk.' At once the man was cured; he picked up his mat and walked" (5:8-9). Let me summarize. Until we do the improbable, God doesn't do the impossible.

Notice the order of Jesus' words:
a. Pick up your mat.
b, Walk.

While lying on the ground, the paralytic could pick up his mat, but to what end? It made no sense to pick it up until he could walk. The man had to be willing to play the part of the fool. What if he picked up the mat, but couldn't walk? Sure, the Scripture says he was cured "at once," but he had no way of knowing he could walk—after 38 years—until he actually got up and tried to walk.

Had Jesus said to walk, and then pick up the mat, it would have made sense. But healing is all about surrender—doing whatever Jesus says, whether it makes sense to us or not. And many times it doesn't. Surrender is the essence of recovery. It is unpacked throughout the 12 Steps. I actually pray the 3rd Step Prayer and 7th Step Prayer each day. Both are prayers of surrender. Without surrender, there can be no healing.

Step 3—Disclosure

Jesus could have visited the man at his home and provided a private healing. Just about any place the paralytic could be found in the course of his normal activities would have been more private. But Jesus strategically chose to heal the man in full view of the crowd. So public was his healing that this immediately spurred a conversation between the man and Jewish leaders who either witnessed the event or heard about it soon after.

Someone needs to know our secrets. The behaviors of porn use and other sexual addictions cripple a man, but it is his secrets that bury him. That is why Beth and I are huge proponents of full clinical disclosures, to be conducted by a Certified Sex Addiction Therapist, along with a polygraph to confirm the details of the written disclosure.

Step 4—Community

Let's pick up the end of the story. "Later Jesus found him at the temple and said to him, 'See, you are well again. Stop sinning or something worse may happen to you.' The man went away and told the Jewish leaders that it was Jesus who had made him well" (John 5:14-15).

Two interesting observations are worth noting. First, notice that Jesus said, "You are well again." This means the man had been able to walk in the past. But how did Jesus know that the man had been able to walk 38 years earlier, before Jesus was even born? This speaks, of course, to the divinity of Christ; he knew what no one had told him.

Second, notice that Jesus found him "at the temple." No one had told the man to go to church; he intuitively felt the need for fellowship. And this is where recovery is sealed. As I tell clients, "The opposite of addiction is not sobriety; it is community." No one gets well and stays well on his own.

Chapter 7
TOOLS YOU CAN USE NOW

Let's get practical. As pastors, we can agree that sexually compulsive behaviors are detrimental to our health—mentally, emotionally, and spiritually. These addictive activities can cost us our marriages, ministries, and more. Yet, millions of us continue to walk in our addiction, rather than in freedom. For many, it comes down to one simple shortcoming—we don't have the tools we need to stay on track. Here, we will suggest 13 very specific tools you can use to stay on the pathway to freedom.

1. Set a date to quit.

Of course, we suggest making that day today. The point is to fix a starting line in your recovery, a point from which you will not turn back. Addiction expert Susan Shapiro suggests several important steps in fixing a date include: telling someone else of your commitment; marking the date on your calendar; attending a recovery meeting on that date; establishing spiritual disciplines on that date.[1] Let's be clear. The best date to quit was five years ago. But the second best date is today. Don't put it off. Draw a line in the sand.

2. Beware of replacement addictions.

Dr. Elizabeth Hartney writes, "Some people find that when they quit or change an addictive behavior, another comes along to replace it. Heavy drinkers and smokers often find themselves overeating and putting on weight. People struggling with sex addiction might find themselves obsessed with exercise. Addictive behaviors have similar neurological and psychological processes and create rewarding feelings and sensations. So replacement addictive behaviors are common among those trying to overcome an addiction."[2]

The key to avoiding replacement addictions is to find satisfaction in the experiences of normal life. These experiences may lack the intensity and high of addictive behaviors, but getting to know and like them can introduce a new level of calm you may not have known before. Sometimes, this takes a lot of work. Identifying alternative experiences may require creativity and the counsel of others.

3. Establish a healthy environment.

Remove as many reminders of your addiction as you can. Delete social media accounts and phone numbers. Get rid of old letters and other objects tied to your addiction. One suggestion is to replace these objects with items that help you feel positive and calm. Fill your refrigerator with wholesome food. Treat yourself to a few good books or DVDs. Even place candles in the room if this helps.[3]

It is imperative to remove as many triggers as possible. And determine to keep certain rules in place. That might mean carrying limited cash, not watching TV by yourself late at night, and avoiding certain channels that present a challenge to your serenity. Anything that is unhealthy needs to be eliminated if at all possible.

4. Make a harmful effects list.

It probably won't feel good to acknowledge all the ways in which your addiction is harming you, but seeing the list on paper will help you resolve to stop the behaviors as soon as possible. Tiffany Douglass offers a simple formula for completing this exercise.[4] This formula follows.

> a. Address why you became addicted in the first place. Ask yourself what it is preventing you from doing or what the addiction is doing for you.
> b. Think about how your addiction has affected your physical health. Are you at greater risk of getting cancer, heart disease, or another illness as a result of your addiction?

Maybe the addiction has already taken a noticeable physical toll.
c. List the ways in which it has hurt you mentally. Are you embarrassed about your addiction? In many cases addictions lead to shame, depression, anxiety, and other mental and emotional issues.
d. How has your addiction affected your relationships with other people? Does it prevent you from spending time with people you love or having enough time to pursue new relationships?
e. Some addictions take a big financial toll. List the amount of money you have spent feeding your addiction every day, week, and month. Determine whether your addiction has affected your job.
f. What daily annoyances are caused by your addiction?

5. Do regular exercise.

One of the most important and accessible addiction recovery tools is physical exercise. Exercise offers drug-free relief from the negative feelings that accompany addiction, such as depression, anxiety, and stress. By exercising in moderation, your body will establish emotional equilibrium and you will begin feeling emotionally, mentally, and, of course, physically well.

Exercise also enhances the detoxification phase of recovery, by ridding any residual chemicals from the body and improving sleep patterns. As part of your recovery journey, try to spend at least 30–60 minutes of exercise a few days a week. Join in extracurricular sports or take walks with friends from your rehab program.

6. Form a support team.

Seek support from your closest friends and loved ones. Let them know how much this means to you. Ask them to help you avoid certain triggers by not including you in watching certain movies or attending certain places. Research confirms that people who have long-term success with overcoming addictions have a strong support group of family and friends who encourage them on a daily basis.[5] This team may consist of other pastors, friends from seminary, or men you have met along the recovery journey. In some cases, you and your wife will want to include couples as part of your team.

7. Try the predicting strategy.

This calls for forethought. Think about what is coming before it comes. The Healing Hearts Counseling Center suggests that you keep a journal to track your behavior patterns. They call this a "prediction journal." The addict should refer to it often, when facing early signs of sexual temptations.[6] Rather than journal on your acting out activities or reflecting on what has transpired throughout the day, the "prediction journal" is where you record your urges before you act on them. This allows you to process what you are feeling before those feelings evolve into fantasy, then acting out.

8. Take some downtime.

As much as it helps to fill your days with sober activities, exercise, and plans to keep busy, it is also important to save some time for yourself. As you move away from addiction, try not to overwhelm yourself with too much at once. A successful recovery program requires personal healing, and personal healing often requires space. It is suggested that you take more naps, relaxing baths, and time off from the rigorous duties at church, even if this means canceling a few appointments.[7] This is really hard for most pastors, who are basically on call 24/7. To take some downtime is not a sin; I would argue that to not take some downtime is.

9. Engage in different kinds of therapy.

Lea Winerman introduces several kinds of therapy for addiction treatment. She says, "Researchers have developed effective behavioral and pharmaceutical therapies to treat addiction—but addiction treatment practice hasn't caught up with the science." She suggests the following examples.[8]
- a. Cognitive behavioral therapy: CBT can help addicted patients overcome their struggles by teaching them to recognize and avoid destructive thoughts and behaviors. A cognitive-behavioral therapist can, for example, teach a client to recognize the triggers that cause his craving for

his drug of choice. The client then learns how to avoid or manage those triggers.

b. Motivational interviewing: This therapy technique involves structured conversations that help clients increase their motivation to overcome addiction. They are taught to focus on the pain and insanity of the addicted lifestyle versus what life could be apart from their acting out.

c.. Contingency management: With this methodology, therapists provide tangible incentives to encourage clients to stay off their drug. These rewards might include work provisions, clinical privileges, or a suggestion of how the client might reward himself for completion of assigned recovery work.

d. Network therapy: Network therapy is a collaboration of addict, therapist, family, and peers working together toward a common goal. This provides social support for the addict at the genesis of his treatment. This is an alternative to intensive treatment at a recovery center, from which the addict then must try to re-engage his former environment. Marc Galanter writes, "A daring approach to therapy puts addicts where they belong—among family and friends. Knowing the effects they have on their loved ones motivates many addicts to live an addiction-free life."[9]

10. Get creative.

British writer John Trogdon suggests ten tools for overcoming addiction. One of those is creativity. Trogdon writes, "Do you like playing music, dancing, drawing, or acting? These art forms are important for a recovering addict because he or she can do them without having to suffer from the side effects of destructive behaviors."[10]

Now is a great time to pick up a new hobby. Chase your passions. Look for something that is fun, healthy, and outside the box. It is especially good to pursue hobbies that are not triggers to past behaviors. It may be a good idea to join a club of some kind, centered on your hobby, in order to build new relationships.

11. Give meditation a try.

Successful recovery requires a stable state of mind. Sometimes, however, intense cravings, prolonged withdrawal symptoms, and mental distress or health disorders can get in the way. That is why addiction experts will recommend meditative techniques to help you press the "pause" button on any stressful reactions, and to restore emotional equilibrium while in recovery. Meditation can come in many different forms.

Dr. Deepak Chopra, in "Overcoming Addictions," writes, "All addictions have one thing in common: their power depends on something external, something out there in the world, something extrinsic to the individual self. Meditating is the opposite, the antithesis, of addictive behavior."[11]

12. The 20-Minute Rule

This is one of the most effective tools I've used in leading men to freedom. It's pretty simple. Most of the time, when the overwhelming urge to act out sweeps over us, we want to immediately cave in and self-medicate. There is a sudden feeling of anxiety. As 12-Step recovery materials tell us, "The only way we knew to be free of it was to do it." Oscar Wilde said, "The only way to get rid of a temptation is to yield to it."[12]

But the urge will pass. We know that the initial demand for self-pleasure will begin to fade in about 20 minutes. The goal, then, is not to stay sober for the next 24 hours, but for the next 24 minutes. After that, the urge will pass. If you act out in that time, you will now live in shame. If you don't act out, you'll live in victory.

13. Do a Recovery Day.

This is something my 12-Step sponsor taught me several years ago. It is one of the best tools you will have in your toolbox. A Recovery Day is a day you spend on yourself, doing several activities that help you to relax, reflect, and reprogram. These may include things such as a hike at a park, trip to a museum, lunch at a new restaurant, reading a good book, meditation, a new recovery group, prayer, reading a new book, or any number of healthy outlets for the stress and pressure that may have built up over time. Elizabeth Grace Sunders is a time management coach and author of *Divine Time Management*. She writes, "To make this happen, you'll need to have resolved that your self-care time is sacred and that you're going to follow through on it. That means eliminating hurdles and putting in items that reinforce positive behaviors."[13]

Chapter 8
THE ROAD BACK

The question that is most asked is, "What disqualifies a pastor from public ministry?" Perhaps a better question would be, "What does a pastor need to do to come back?" By "come back," I am not speaking of a man's return to the pulpit, but his return to kingdom service on whatever level is deemed appropriate. The pastor's personal recovery matters far more than whether he ever steps back onto a public platform. We will consider several aspects of a pastor's road back from the ditch of addiction.

Four Things About Restoration

We can't have a book for pastors without including alliteration at some point. So here we go. As we consider the various aspects of the road back, there are a few basic themes that underscore effective recovery. They combine to pour the foundation on which successful restoration may take place. Each of these principles is equally important.

1. Restoration is a promise.

One of God's magnificent and precious promises is found in Jeremiah 30:17. "For I will restore you to health, and I will heal you of your wounds." Ministers get wounded, whether self-inflicted or not. Often, for the sake of the people in the church, pastors let their personal health and emotional wellness go until they get so frustrated and discouraged that they can't see straight. Some clergy become so tired and stay so weary that they think this is the way ministry is supposed to be. Jesus said, "Come to me, all who are weary and heavy laden, and I will give you rest" (Matthew 11:28-30).

2. Restoration is a process.

There can be no microwave restoration. Indeed, God heals, and he can touch us and restore us in a second when faith is present. But renewing a weary soul and restoring a wounded heart takes time. As Steve Boll writes, "Process is not a four-letter word."[1] Process is our friend. "He restoreth my soul" is a time tested and proven process that insures complete healing and wholeness. We are so busy as ministers that we miss full restoration, and settle for partial renewal. We need more than a tune-up. What we need is a complete overhaul. Restoration is for life. In fact, I would argue that restoration and renewal are needed by every pastor regularly.

3. Restoration is personal.

Restoration is intensely individual. The twenty-third Psalm is full of personal pronouns. For example, "He restores my soul." Because we are unique and special, God has a tailor-made plan of renewal for every pastor. In the ministry, there have been times when I needed restoration. Whether anyone else did or not, I certainly did. The Lord gently invited me to come. If I ignored the invitation, he made me come! Circumstances drove me to the tranquil, restful places. There he directed me to the Scripture I needed. He filled me with his Spirit. He strengthened my inner man. The richest times come when he restores our souls.

4. Restoration is powerful.

In Psalm 92:10 we read that David jubilantly declared, "I have been anointed with fresh oil." Restoration restores people to a life of power—God's power of love operating through the Holy Spirit. Oh, how we as pastors need "fresh oil!" God's anointing for daily ministry tasks is not optional if we are to be fruitful.

In Jeremiah 31, we find Judah's powerful restoration to the Lord. Take special note of the benefits and blessings God bestowed upon his restored people. Restoration takes powerless people and pastors and turns them into powerhouses for the

Lord. Nothing serves as a more definitive example of God's redemption than this.

The Stages of Recovery

"Recovery is a process of personal growth in which each stage has its own risks of relapse and its own developmental tasks to reach the next stage."[2] One of the things I repeat often is that relapse is not an event, but a process. The same is true of recovery. The road back is long, not short; winding, not straight; difficult, not easy. While the road back is gradual and often dotted with unexpected speed bumps and potholes, there are stages through which the addict must pass. Different experts in the field offer various versions of these stages, but we will suggest a simple pattern that is consistent with the basic tenets of recovery.

1. Abstinence Stage

Most agree that this is the initial stage of recovery, and generally lasts for one to two years. The focus in this stage is dealing with the cravings and not returning to one's addictive behaviors. These are some of the tasks in the abstinence stage:

- Accept that you have an addiction.
- Practice honesty in life.
- Develop coping skills for dealing with cravings.
- Become active in self-help groups.
- Practice self-care and saying no.
- Understand the stages of relapse.
- Get rid of friends who are using.
- Understand the dangers of cross addiction.

2. Repair Stage

In the second stage of recovery, the main task is to repair the damage caused by addiction. This period may last two to three years. It is common to feel emotions of failure in this stage, as we focus on the damage of our past. Dr. Steven M. Melemis offers several developmental tasks within this stage.[3]

- Use cognitive therapy to overcome negative self-labeling and catastrophizing.
- Understand that individuals are not their addiction.
- Repair relationships and make amends when possible.
- Start to feel comfortable with being uncomfortable.
- Improve self-care and make it an integral part of recovery.
- Develop a balanced and healthy lifestyle.
- Continue to engage in self-help groups.
- Develop more healthy alternatives to using.

3. Growth Stage

In the growth stage, we begin to move forward. This usually begins between three and five years into sobriety. It is now that the addict begins to deal with family issues and past trauma. This involves heavy lifting in therapy and reflection. Dr. Melemis writes, "The tasks of this stage are similar to the tasks that non-addicts face in everyday life."[4] These are the tasks of this recovery stage.

- Identify and repair negative thinking and self-destructive patterns.
- Understand how negative familial patterns have been passed down.
- Challenge fears with cognitive therapy.
- Set healthy boundaries.
- Begin to give back and help others.
- Reevaluate one's lifestyle periodically.

Targeted Progressive Restoration

Restoration is God's "Amen" to any story of a fallen saint. What the enemy intends for evil, God can turn for good. But a process must be followed.

Chris Fabry, with Focus on the Family, has produced a helpful process, which he calls a "targeted progressive restoration."[5] Fabry's emphasis is on maintaining the proper priorities in the restoration process. Too often, the question becomes "How quickly can I get back into ministry?" rather than "How do I renew my relationship with God, my family, and my congregation?"

Impatience is the enemy of restoration. It takes time to restore those who have fallen. It takes time to prove the authenticity of repentance. And it takes time to rebuild broken relationships.

Fabry offers the following five steps in the progression of restoration.

1. Authentic and intimate relationship with God
2. Intimate and trusting relationship with family
3. Church fellowship with no ministry responsibilities
4. Good reputation within the community
5. Possibility of ministry

Five Things Addicts Tell Themselves

One of the keys to a dramatic comeback is a change in our thinking. There are several dangerous mindsets addicts must avoid. These are common lies they tell themselves, rather than facing the difficulty of true recovery. Until they confront these erroneous patterns, addicts will not get well. Following are five lines addicts tell themselves.

1. I can stop anytime I want.

Keep in mind, it is the addiction that makes the addict feel in control. So to him it makes perfect sense to state a position of total control when he is actually out of control. The addict reasons, "Since I choose to act out these behaviors, I can choose to stop—anytime." This is one of the most difficult obstacles to reaching a loved one who is a porn addict. As long as he thinks he is in control, he will not surrender.

2. If everyone would leave me alone, I'd be okay.

The addict convinces himself that he is not the problem. Pastors are especially vulnerable here. Their heightened moral code does not allow them to recognize this sin within them. Life becomes one big exercise of compartmentalization. Pastors reason that their issues are between them and God; others should just get off their backs.

3. It's my life, and it's my choice.

A close friend used this line on me a number of years ago. "It's my life to mess up if I want to." That would be true, except for one thing. Every addict's mistakes affect many others. This is especially true for pastors. What is done in secret always comes out, and its effects are traumatic. One writer said it like this: "Addiction stories happen every day in the lives of thousands of communities across America and the rest of the world. It's clear that addiction affects everyone who knows the addict—not only the addict himself."[6]

4. Recovery is worse than addiction.

One reason pastors often live in secrecy isn't that they are trying to hide their struggle; it's that they are hiding their recovery. The pastor who has studied for years to attain his degrees, then puts in the hard work of leading churches for several years, if not decades, has climbed a hill too far from which to fall. Eventually, he reaches an impasse. He must go all in for recovery or just give up. Sadly, many give up.

5. Getting help means I'm weak.

"God plus one equals a majority." "God is all you need." "I am an overcomer." What pastor hasn't said these things? I can relate. That was me for 31 years. I prayed hard and tried harder. But the more I swung, the more I missed. Eventually, I had to admit it—I couldn't do this on my own. The need for others isn't a sign of weakness, but a confirmation that we were simply created for community.

Five Steps to Restoration

Our point here is not to say that every pastor should be restored to public ministry. This section is not for the church, but the pastor. We will propose five steps the pastor must take in order to be considered for restoration in public ministry. And if the church decides he has permanently disqualified himself from such consideration, these are steps toward spiritual health and restoration which he should take anyway. Overcoming the devastation of sexual sin will be the hardest—and perhaps most rewarding—thing a pastor will ever accomplish.

Step 1—Early on, do as little as possible.

This may sound unproductive, but it will save you great pain in the future. At the beginning of a crisis, all the forces of our emotions will try to dictate our next moves. Don't react. Listen to your feelings, but don't follow them blindly. Early in recovery, it is important to not make any life-altering decisions. Yes, you need to get into therapy, some kind of support group, and hard recovery work. But don't make decisions today that can be made tomorrow—about your church, position, marriage, or whom to include in your story. There will be plenty of time for that later.

Step 2—Evaluate the root of your problem.

Sexual addiction is not a bad problem as much as it is a bad solution. Spend time with a Certified Sex Addiction Therapist, working to isolate your triggers. Look into your past. Ask questions about your trauma, abuse, and isolation. Consider family history. Ask what pain you were trying to soothe with the use of porn. Why were you seeking to self-medicate? What unresolved anger issues persist? In what areas have your dreams gone unfulfilled? How do you measure success? Consider other factors that may have played a part in your addiction, such as burnout, unhealthy boundaries, and conflict within the church. Dig deep, then dig some more. Think of your porn problem as weeds in your garden. You can ignore those weeds, cover them with mulch, or trim their tops off. But until you dig down deep and pull the weeds out by their roots, they will only return.

Step 3—Work on a plan of restoration.

Only after your family is healing and you are in a good place with your personal recovery should you even think about saving your ministry. But when the right time comes, your road back will mean considering the steps you can take to re-engage in ministry, if you have lost your position. If you have not lost your ministry position, you still need to be restored spiritually and emotionally. Such restoration begins with biblical repentance. You must seek reconciliation with those you have hurt, starting with your family. You may need to meet with church leaders, to express your regret and offer amends. Own what you have done.

Step 4—Come back in stages.

Let's assume you have lost your ministry position, and are confident that God wants to restore you to public ministry. Do it in stages. That means rebuilding trust. This takes time. Before you return to pulpit ministry, lead a small group. Take on a volunteer ministry position of some kind. Put yourself under someone else's authority.

For me—and your story will be different—it meant backing away from any public ministry for one year. I drove for Uber and Lyft. I delivered groceries and drove elderly people to doctor's appointments. I did some writing and behind the scenes ministry. I joined a local church and became a greeter, then head greeter. I served (still serve) on church committees. I slowly accepted more preaching requests.

We only launched our recovery ministry—*There's Still Hope*—once I had five years of solid recovery. And I lead with my weaknesses. I don't hide my addiction from any church that may want to use me in some way. When I lost my 31-year pastoral ministry, I never dreamed I'd be back in public ministry of any kind again. And it did not come quickly, but in stages. Any road back should always come in stages.

Step 5—Celebrate all wins.

The road back may not mean you become a pastor again. It just means God isn't through with you yet. Your set-back becomes God's set-up. The Sovereign God was not surprised by what happened with you. He will use you because of your past, not despite your past. I am convinced that every church that ever dismisses a staff person because of his sin should strive to work with that staff person, to see him get the help he needs and help pave the road back to meaningful ministry—whether at their church or in a nonvisible ministry. The church should bring their pastor back to pray over him. They should celebrate his progress in recovery. Pastor, if your church doesn't help you celebrate your wins, find someone else who will.

Final Reflections

It is not my goal to answer the question of whether a fallen pastor can return to public ministry again. There are so many faith traditions as well as shades of "fallen" to be considered that it would be impossible to give a blanket statement, a "one size fits all" response. But a final reflection of the subject is in order. I like the way ethicist Russell Moore addresses this subject in his article, "What to Do When a Pastor Falls."[7] Moore writes, "Sometimes I find myself fuming after a leader has fallen at the stupidity of it. Why would he risk his family for this? Why would he jeopardize the witness of Christ? The reason I am so frustrated is because of my inadequate doctrine of sin. It doesn't matter what I confess in creedal documents or teach from pulpits. All sin is irrational and self-destructive. If we don't get that, we don't know what sin is. My reaction is a reminder to myself of how much I need the sanctifying presence of the Spirit."

The sins of others are always more shocking to us than our own sins. We tend to judge others by their actions, but we judge ourselves by our intentions. If we didn't intend to hurt anyone, we are not guilty of hurting anyone, we reason.

The harshest critic of fallen leaders—insert name of your favorite fallen leader to criticize—would be wise to consider the biblical record. *God only uses fallen men and women*. The Bible doesn't offer a romantic view of leaders, the way we might expect as readers. The prophets and matriarchs and apostles are all presented with glaring flaws. Moses saw the glory of Israel's God in the flaming bush, saw the fire of Sinai, and fell anyway. Peter heard the Sermon on the Mount first-hand, washed his beard out in the stream of Judea alongside Jesus Christ himself—and still denied he ever knew him by the charcoal fire. Russell Moore writes, "The fact that we are shocked when our leaders fall is a demonstration that we are not nearly as realistic about human nature—and about spiritual warfare—as the Bible is."[8]

Chapter 9
EIGHT GUARDRAILS THAT WORK

In his groundbreaking book, *Out of the Shadows*, Patrick Carnes offers a poignant warning to sex addicts everywhere with four simple words: "The future is conditional."[1] In other words, relapse is a choice. It seems like we read about another pastor falling into sexual sin every week. For many pastors, they simply fell asleep at the wheel, and before they knew it, they were tumbling over the cliff. The answer is to put guardrails firmly in place. I'm talking about cement guardrails, not the cheap metal variety. And when you put your guardrails in place, pastor, stay as far from them as you can.

When you drive up a winding, treacherous mountain road, you will hopefully have a guardrail between the road and the cliff. Unless you have a rock for a brain, you strive to keep your car as far from that guardrail as possible. The point of the guardrail is not to draw us as close to danger as we can possibly get, but to keep us back. Likewise, your sexual guardrails should scream, "Stay back! Don't come near!" Any time you brush up against a guardrail, even if you don't fall off the side of the mountain, you will sustain significant damage.

Before You Get Started

If you are ready to jump in and start erecting guardrails, congratulations! You are about to take a giant step forward in your restoration. But there are a few important guidelines that are helpful in taking that big step. These are principles that will guide the never ending process of building guardrails.

1. Start with non-sexual guardrails.

For most of us, we think only about the boundaries that will secure our sexual purity. We become consumed with the things that will protect us from ourselves, dangerous situations, and unnecessary triggers. Nick Stumbo, Executive Director for Pure Desire, says, "The best guardrails I have don't address my past addiction at all. They address all the patterns that were part of my behaviors."[2] Stumbo identifies such challenges as procrastination, wasting time online, and channel surfing as patterns that need guardrails. It is important that we practice enough self-reflection to be able to recognize the dangers that will fight for our attention and passion.

2. Guardrails must be immovable.

Guardrails cannot be effective if we make them flexible. Guardrails must be made of steel, not plastic. I've seen it happen dozens of times. Guy sets guardrail. He will not be alone with a woman other than his wife. Guy sticks to his plan. Until Girl walks in. Not just any Girl, but attractive Girl who works down the hall in a nearby office. Girl isn't asking for a hot date, just a few minutes of "wise counsel" from Guy. Next thing you know, Guy has gone off the cliff.

All guardrails must be taken seriously—sufficient sleep, good diet, exercise, no late night movies, no phone in the rest room, etc. It is the five percent of the time that we let things slide that we lose it all. Write your guardrails in stone, not sand.

3. Pick positive guardrails.

Nick Stumbo writes, "One danger of guardrails is that they all become a giant 'no' stamped on our lives. What we need is holistic guardrails to help us know where the 'yes' is in our lives."[3] Guardrails need to be about starting things, not just stopping things. Look for healthy activities you can begin, not just for unhealthy behaviors you should end. One way to define these guardrails is to think in terms of the three circles exercise from 12-Step work. Our inner circle behaviors break our sobriety, while our middle circle activities push us toward relapse. It is the outer circle behaviors that secure our sobriety and keep us in a healthy space. These are the kinds of proactive guardrails that keep us from going off the side of the road.

4. Don't listen to curiosity.

It seems like I read somewhere that curiosity killed the cat. While I'm not sure I've ever actually witnessed that, I have seen many pastors fall because of curiosity. It is curiosity that leads us to the wrong movie, website, app, and relationship. We become like Lot, of the Old Testament. It was when he "cast his tent toward Sodom" (Genesis 13:12) that he got into trouble. Lot never dreamed he'd end up in Sodom. And the enemy went along with him. Remember, we don't fall; we slide. Relapse is a process, not an event. It is when we play the curiosity game that we move beyond the guardrails of our recovery.

Eight Guardrails that Work

You can find dozens of good resources for guardrails that will greatly enhance your recovery efforts. Our focus here will be on those which I believe will be the most helpful to you as a pastor. Don't receive this as a complete list. There will be a couple of guardrails here that may not be especially useful to you, and there will certainly be several guardrails that you will need to embrace, which will not be on this list. It is wise to include your therapist, sponsor, or another trusted recovery leader in compiling your personalized list of guardrails. That said, let's dive into a few good guardrails.

1. Get a genuine accountability partner.

The mistake many men make is to ask a friend to be an accountability partner without ever detailing what that entails. This person must be willing to ask the hard questions and to say things that the addict may not like. It may not be best for you to tap a friend you are particularly close to, as the nature of this relationship will be different from that of a typical friendship. If you are serious about accountability, you will offer complete transparency. It is even recommended by some that you allow this person to see your bank statements, credit card statements, internet browsing history, text messages, and emails.[4] Of course, you will need to adapt your own accountability agreement to meet your specific needs and triggers.

Robert Weiss, in *Sex Addiction 101*, identifies ten requirements for a successful accountability relationship. He contends, "Establishing and developing this accountability relationship is an essential element of growing and maintaining sexual recovery and healing." His ten keys to making this work are found below.[5]

a. Promise to reach out immediately if you feel triggered to act out sexually.
b. Promise to reach out immediately if you actually do act out sexually.
c. Throw away all physical material related to the problem.
d. Go through your computer, laptop, tablet, smartphones, etc., deleting any and all files, emails, texts, sexts, bookmarks, profiles, apps, and contact information related to your addiction.
e. Cancel any sex addiction-related memberships to websites, apps, and/or brick-and-mortar establishments, along with any credit cards you've used to pay for these memberships, to make sure they don't automatically renew.
f. Commit that you will stay away from "gray area" activities.
g. Commit to only using digital devices when others can see you.
h. Create reminders of why you want to change your behavior.
i. Purchase and install parental control software, such as Covenant Eyes.
j. Create and implement a plan for sexual sobriety.

Your accountability partner needs to be given permission—by you—to ask the tough questions. "Have you looked at porn this week?" "How is your quiet time going?" "What are you doing to build your marriage?" "Have you texted any women without your wife's knowledge this week?" "Have you had any personal conversations with any women in your church this week?" "Are you doing your recovery work?"

2. Embrace the "Man Code."

I recommend Dennis Swanberg's book, *The Man Code*. "Swan" takes us on a fascinating journey back in time. He demonstrates how Jesus had certain numbers in his life. He had the *one*, which represented his walk with God. Jesus had the *three*, who were his closest friends—Peter, James, and John. Then he had the *12*—his small group, which consisted of the apostles. Add to that the *120*, which represents the church. Finally, Jesus had the *5,000*, which is the community. You need all of these in your life, pastor, if you are to maintain balance.

3. Read the Bible differently.

As a pastor, you have probably used the Bible more as a tool for ministry than as a source of personal strength. Author Brandon Kelley writes, "It's one thing to read the Bible, it's another thing to read it with a receptive heart. In other words, when you read the Bible, whether that be in your personal devotion time or preparing to preach or teach, receive the words as for you before you ever try to share them with someone else. Your heart needs to be in the position of receiving the truth of the Bible."[6] The Bible needs to be a tool for personal growth, not just for you to do your job.

4. Pray with purpose.

There is not a greater guardrail than simply spending time with God—for the purpose of spending time with God. Brandon Kelley writes, "A pastoral guardrail you can't miss is going to God in prayer with all of you on the table. Regular prayer that is authentic, transparent, and raw is vital for the health of your walk with God as well as your sustainability as a leader."[7] Lay it all out to God in prayer—your temptations, failings, fantasies, fears, shortcomings, inadequacies, and pain. Seek God more than you seek his answers.

5. Practice the Modesto Manifesto.

In 1948, Billy Graham began a series of evangelistic meetings in Modesto, California, along with his ministry team, comprised of Cliff Barrows, George Beverly Shea, and Grady Wilson. Through a series of conversations about ministry life and its challenges, the group met together in Modesto and resolved to uphold the highest standard of biblical morality and integrity.

In the following excerpt from his autobiography, *Just As I Am*, Billy Graham described the details about the resolutions these men made in terms of financial integrity, sexual morality, publicity, and partnership with the local church. These resolutions became known as the "Modesto Manifesto."[8]

"One afternoon during the Modesto meetings, I called the team together to discuss the problem. Then I asked them to go to their rooms for an hour and list all the problems they could think of that evangelists and evangelism encountered.

"When they returned, the lists were remarkably similar, and in a short amount of time, we made a series of resolutions or commitments among ourselves that would guide us in our future evangelistic work. In reality, it was more of an informal understanding among ourselves—a shared commitment to do all we could do to uphold the Bible's standard of absolute integrity and purity for evangelists.

"The first point on our combined list was money. Nearly all evangelists at the time—including us—were supported by love offerings taken at the meetings. The temptation to wring as much money as possible out of an audience, often with strong emotional appeals, was too great for some evangelists. In addition, there was little or no accountability for finances. It was a system that was easy to abuse—and led to the charge that evangelists were in it only for the money.

"I had been drawing a salary from YFC (Youth for Christ) and turning all offerings from YFC meetings over to YFC committees, but my new independent efforts in citywide campaigns required separate finances. In Modesto we determined to do all we could to avoid financial abuses and to downplay the offering and depend as much as possible on money raised by the local committees in advance.

"The second item on the list was the danger of sexual immorality. We all knew of evangelists who had fallen into immorality while separated from their families by travel. We pledged among ourselves to avoid any situations that would have even the appearance of compromise or suspicion. From that day on, I did not travel, meet, or eat alone with a woman other than my wife. We determined that the Apostle Paul's mandate to the young pastor Timothy would be ours as well: 'Flee youthful lusts' (2 Timothy 2:22, KJV).

"Our third concern was the tendency of many evangelists to carry on their work apart from the local church, even to criticize local pastors and churches openly and scathingly. We were convinced, however, that this was not only counterproductive but also wrong from the Bible's standpoint. We were determined to cooperate with all who would cooperate with us in the public proclamation of the Gospel, and to avoid an anti-church or anti-clergy attitude.

"The fourth and final issue was publicity. The tendency among some evangelists was to exaggerate their successes or to claim higher attendance numbers than they really had. This likewise discredited evangelism and brought the whole enterprise under suspicion. It often made the press so suspicious of evangelists that they refused to take notice of their work. In Modesto we committed ourselves to integrity in our publicity and our reporting."

6. Hit the reset button as needed.

It's a fact—you will sin at some point. You will flirt with old habits and fantasies. You will let your mind go places that are dark and dangerous. You may even commit an action that resets your sobriety. The key is to decide—in advance—that none of this will end the journey. Commit to getting back up in the event of a fall of any size. Make sure you have surrounded yourself with the right people so that when the time does come for you to confess a failing of some kind, you will be prepared to do it.

7. Get in a group.

Research confirms, "The community reinforcement approach has been used for decades and seeks to emphasize the benefits of abstinence and reduce the positive reinforcement associated with addictive behaviors."[9]

I'm familiar with reasons to not attend 12-Step meetings... They are not Christ-centered, the readings are repetitive, etc. But I have found five great 12-Step sayings that offer hope and guidance. Though none of them are biblical, per se, none is unbiblical. I find them helpful.

You're only as sick as your secrets. Recovery begins with honesty. This honesty starts with sharing the problem with someone else. When we keep our addiction to ourselves, this perpetuates shame, and the cycle of addiction continues. That is because shame is rooted in a feeling of worthlessness and feeds isolation. There is within each of us the need to be both fully known and completely accepted. Until we share our secrets, we can experience neither of these. Honesty breaks the cycle of shame and fosters community.

Take what you like and leave the rest. Pastors are trained to examine everything. We don't accept theological assumptions without careful and thorough examination. And that's a good thing. So it is natural that we would pick apart the theology of any 12-Step program. This is a huge mistake. Part of the genius of the original AA literature (from 1939) is its own acknowledgment that no one would be expected to blindly accept every word written on every page of the Big Book (of AA). Not everything in any particular program will apply to you, and some of what you read will probably not align with your belief system. That's okay. Don't attach too much to what you don't agree with. What works for me is a simple prayer I try to remember to breathe to God at the start of every 12-Step meeting that I attend: "Lord, may I hear just one thing in the next hour that can help my recovery today." After attending over 800 "secular" 12-Step meetings, that prayer has been answered every time.

Acronyms, acronyms, and more acronyms. I admit this can become tiresome. When you first hear some of these little acronyms, you feel like a complete outsider to the group. Some members throw these around as if they have an inside track to a foreign language. But they are good if you use them. So here goes.

H.A.L.T.: People tend to be triggered when they are hungry, angry, lonely, or tired.

S.L.I.P.: A slip happens when sobriety loses its priority.

F.E.A.R.: Fear is the result of frustration, ego, anxiety, and resentment.

The program works if you work it. You hear this at every meeting. The point is that recovery is active, not passive. You don't find sobriety by just showing up. I tell clients all the time, "If you are 90 percent in, you are 100 percent out." To "work it" means attending meetings consistently, working the Steps rigorously, and working with one's sponsor wholeheartedly.

One day at a time. This phrase has helped countless numbers of people recover from their various addictions. It emphasizes a focus on daily examination of where we stand with our recovery. Many people get discouraged that they only have short-term sobriety, but in a sense, that's all any of us ever have. Sobriety is a daily thing. When we start thinking too far ahead, we are in trouble. As I say in my Freedom Groups, no matter how far you have gone down the road, the ditch is still just as close on either side.

8. Get on Covenant Eyes.

One of your greatest guardrails will be protection on your tablet, laptop, or cell phone. For the vast majority of us, this is an indispensable tool for recovery, especially for the first full year of total sobriety. Several organizations provide a level of protection, but I will focus on just one, which we have found to be especially helpful for dozens of our clients.

I am a huge proponent of Covenant Eyes. This is a service which provides a layer of accountability for all of your devices. For a very reasonable cost, you can sign up, and be ready to go within minutes. You will need an accountability partner who will agree to be your ally. After you submit your information (name, email, etc.), Covenant Eyes will send a request to your ally, asking him if he is willing to receive your daily reports. (If you prefer, the reports can go out every three days or once a week.) Then, your ally will receive these simple reports by email, notifying him of any questionable activity on any of your devices. For more information, simply review the Covenant Eyes website.[10]

A Word from Andy Stanley

It would be hard to discuss guardrails without including an excerpt from Andy Stanley, whose book, Guardrails: Avoiding Regrets in Your Life, is both informative and challenging. Andy writes, "When was the last time you took a good, long look at a guardrail? It was probably the last time you needed one. Guardrails aren't much to look at. They're mostly dull gray metal with dents and dings that remind us of why they're there—to protect us. That's why you'd rather not notice them, because noticing a guardrail usually means you've just smashed your car into it. And yet, when that happens, how grateful are you that the guardrail is there? Sure, it did a number on your fender and grillwork, but things could've been much worse. Guardrails protect us from what lurks on the other side. The danger zone. You never see guardrails on long, flat stretches of road. They're in the sharp curves and along the sheer cliffs. Yes, they can dent your bumper and bust your headlight. But all that lies on the other side of the guardrail could do far greater damage."[11]

Make Your Laptop Safe

For most pastors (men, in general), the computer or laptop presents the greatest danger to sobriety. It is just too easy to reach over, turn it on, and go crazy. I read a statistic recently that said that 43 percent of all internet users look at porn on their laptops. So what can we do about it?

I had an interesting conversation with a man who was struggling with his sobriety. His biggest challenge seemed to come at night, usually when he was up late. He would reach for his laptop, look up porn, and masturbate. This pattern became very predictable, so he asked for help.

I suggested that he put his laptop in the trunk of his car by 10:00 each night, then park his car on the other end of his apartment complex.

"But I don't think my laptop will be safe in the trunk of my car, as anyone who really wants to can break into my car."

I responded, "You're right. Your laptop may not be safe in the trunk of your car. But we know it's not safe in your bedroom."

Why Guardrails Fail

You can have the best guardrails in place and have the best intentions, but still fly off the cliff. As I look back over my years of recovery, I recognize several mistakes from my early experiences with guardrails. There were lessons I had to learn the hard way. I have had great sponsors throughout my recovery, but I'm not sure any of them really educated me on the reasons many guardrails fail. I share the following examples from my own experience.

1. Too many guardrails were only about avoidance.

To the novice, it is easy to fall into the trap of simply not doing "bad" things. The idea is to try harder, block certain websites, avoid R-rated movies, and not spend time with certain people or in certain places. While this may be helpful at times, this strategy does not address attitude. It is easy to become prideful over the things we don't do. But I learned that avoidance wasn't enough to keep me sober.

2. I didn't tell enough other people about my guardrails.

Guardrails shared become far more effective. I often made a list of my guardrails, but because I didn't tell anyone else what they were, it became easy to ignore them. I am a planner by nature, so coming up with a recovery plan came easy. What didn't come easy was accountability. Until we are willing to let others in on our guardrails, we will be far more likely to compromise our personal commitments.

3. Some of my guardrails were too narrow.

We need to erect guardrails that keep us out of our middle circle behaviors, not just our inner circle behaviors. Early in my recovery, my guardrails were completely focused on avoiding my bottom line behaviors which broke my sobriety. But as my recovery has strengthened, I have shifted my focus toward activities that simply make me vulnerable to a fall. For example, if I have conversations with women without my wife's knowledge or watch certain movies by myself, I am not breaking my sobriety. But what I am doing is setting myself up for a possible fall.

Lesson from a King

"Hezekiah set to work resolutely and built up all the wall that was broken down and raised towers upon it, and outside it he built another wall" (2 Chronicles 32:5).

One of the greatest guardrails is found in the little-known story of King Hezekiah. The story of the wall he commissioned 2,700 years ago brings great relevance to recovery today.

In the rubble that filled the streets of Jerusalem following the 1967 Six-Day War, archaeologists scrambled to see what the bombs had unearthed before the bulldozers came through and smoothed over the past once again. One group of archaeologists found a very old wall, so deep below the present-day city that it could hardly be called a wall anymore.

The wall they found was older that the Ottoman Old City wall or the Wailing Wall. This ancient wall dates to the reign of King Hezekiah, and it represents one of those rare and satisfying occasions when archaeology uncovers something that everyone but the most hardened skeptics can celebrate.

This wall had been enormous at its erection. The remains were found to be 20 feet wide and ten feet tall in some places, still. But why was it built in the first place?

Hezekiah found himself on the wrong side of Sennacherib, King of Assyria, when he stopped paying tribute to the Assyrians in order to secure the safety of his people. At that time, Jerusalem's urban population extended beyond the old walls of the city that had stood for generations. As Hezekiah began to prepare for a certain siege at the hands of Sennacherib, he knew the old walls were no longer sufficient to protect his people. This meant a new wall of defense needed to be built.

The Bible records the story three times, each offering unique details. But it is the Chronicles account that identifies this second wall of defense. As the Assyrian army slowly approached Jerusalem, destroying most of the other Judean cities on the way, Jerusalem's citizens sacrificed their houses to build the wall so they could survive. Isaiah offers some detail: "You counted the houses of Jerusalem, and you broke down the houses to fortify the wall" (Isaiah 22:11). Even today, tourists can view the foundations from the houses which were torn down in order to use their materials to build the second wall of Jerusalem.

When the Assyrian army finally arrived outside the new wall, Sennacherib's representative was sent to scare the defenders on the wall into surrendering, reminding them that no city had ever survived the Assyrian siege.

The messenger asked, "On what are you trusting, that you endure the siege in Jerusalem? Is not Hezekiah misleading you, that he may give you over to die by famine and by thirst, when he tells you, 'The Lord will deliver us from the hand of the King of Assyria?'"

But God's children stood firm, the wall served its purpose, and their lives were preserved.

Perhaps your old wall isn't enough anymore. Perhaps it's time for you to build a second wall of defense.

If You Are Married

One of the most effective guardrails for married sex addicts is to check in with their wives. Don't misunderstand—your wife should not be your accountability partner. But it is critical to let your wife know how your recovery is coming and about any major struggles or threats you are facing. There are many ways to do this, but we recommend the FASTT Check-in process, which we learned from my mentor, Dr. Milton Magness.[12]

A FASTT Check-in is a brief weekly process in which the addict gives his or her partner a progress report concerning recovery. The purpose of this check-in is to keep the spouse informed about the addict's recovery activities, normalize talking about recovery topics, and allow both partners to be alert for signs that recovery needs to receive greater priority.

Magness recommends that addicts continue to check in for at least three years following disclosure, or for three years following a slip or relapse. These are the responsibility of the sex addict to initiate. The check-ins only take about ten minutes to complete. It is important for the couple to establish a day and time for this conversation each week. The FASTT Check-in will cover five points.

1. Feelings

This is where the check-in starts. The addict describes his current feelings. Typically, the addict will share four or five feelings during this part of the check-in. This isn't easy for most men, as they have been taught that real men don't share their feelings. Rarely does a man get through this part of the process easily, at first. It takes time for this to become more comfortable.

2. Activities in recovery

For this part of the check-in, the recovering addict has the opportunity to talk about all of the tasks he completed that week in order to support recovery. If the individual is actively working on recovery, the list will be extensive. Some of these activities that will be included are therapy sessions, attendance at meetings, and recovery work, such as going through the 12 Steps. While the addict cannot talk about the work others do in 12-Step meetings, he can tell his mate about his own 12-Step work. This sharing process will likely be uncomfortable at first, but it becomes more natural with time. This is essential for the spouse to build confidence in the legitimacy of her husband's recovery work.

3. Sobriety or slip statement

The third section of the check-in calls for a sobriety statement from the addict. This should include his sobriety date, plus any slip or relapse. The addict will simply tell his spouse whether or not he has remained sober in the last week, and if not, what happened. This can be viewed as a mini-disclosure. Pastor, your wife needs to know if you are really sober this week—no holding back.

4. Threats

Here, you cover the major threats to your sobriety in the past week (since your last check-in). This is when you will talk about your triggers. Here, caution is called for. Your wife doesn't need to know every fantasy or temptation that comes your way—unless they become a major threat to your sobriety. When you are teetering on the brink of relapse, it is critical that your wife knows it.

5. Tools

If you aren't facing major threats to your sobriety, tell your spouse the tools you are using to stay on track. If you are facing major threats to your sobriety, still tell your spouse what tools you are using. These may include the 3-second rule, 20-minute miracle, or any number of tools you will find in this book, and others.

A Personal Conviction

As I think of putting guardrails in place, I will share a personal conviction. This is from an area other than sexual addiction, but I share it to make a larger point. The subject is alcohol use. I choose to abstain, for reasons I will offer below. Don't misunderstand—I am not saying that God wants you to abstain from all alcohol use. I fully recognize that some of the most godly people I know, who have made this a matter of prayer, are completely at ease with drinking alcoholic beverages in moderation. But my story will hopefully relate to your sex addiction guardrails.

A recent study by the National Institute for Health found that exposing alcohol to adolescents may interrupt the key process of brain development, possibly leading to mild cognitive impairment as well as to an escalation in drinking. In the same study, in conjunction with the National Institute on Alcohol Abuse and Alcoholism, it was found that underage drinking is more likely to kill young people than all other drugs combined.[13]

This is just one example of the possible negative impact of alcohol use. And while this study only applies to underage drinkers, that is exactly why I cite this study (rather than multiple studies on the danger of adult drinking). Just this one example—the danger of underage drinking—is enough to give me pause. I wrestle with the example I would be setting for those around me. It is easier for me to just abstain. Problem solved.

Andy Stanley shares the same sentiment, as do many others, of course. The general reasoning is that if we allow ourselves to drink "a little," we have thereby put ourselves at far more risk to alcohol abuse than if we never drink at all.

It's called guardrails. Again, this is my personal conviction; it works for me. For some, abstinence from all TV works. Others have disavowed the use of smart phones and computers. These are all good guardrails—for some.

Chapter 10
AVOIDING RELAPSE

When the broken vessel is put back together, he is not out of the woods. Looming over the horizon is potential trouble. It's called "relapse." As we tell clients almost daily, "It doesn't matter how far you travel down the road of recovery; the ditch is still just as close on either side of the road." A study by Harvard University found that relapse after five years of sobriety is "very rare,"[1] but never impossible.

While we don't have extensive data on the rates of relapse, most studies agree that even the most successful treatment plans have a disappointing relapse rate. About 50 percent of those who complete an intensive program of four to twelve weeks relapse within 12 weeks.[2] Sadly, even with dozens of respected recovery programs available, there is no standard relapse prevention program that has been established.

Despite its challenges, relapse prevention must be an essential part of addiction recovery. Frequent relapses may prevent individuals from progressing in overcoming their addictions. Although relatively little is known about brain functioning in addiction recovery, sustained abstinence seems to allow time for the brain to resume normal functioning that can lay the foundation for long-term success.[3]

Read This First!

We will take a look at the three stages of relapse. But first, we need to consider what comes first. Before any of us ever step into the initial stage of relapse, we walk through what has been called by many researchers the "Pre-Contemplation Stage." This is the period of activity that occurs before any form of relapse begins to take shape. Author Ben Lesser describes it like this: "As the consequences of the behaviors increase and the frequency increases, the dependency increases. Pre-occupation is a phase of relapse prevention done by people who believe they ought to be in rehabilitation, even if they think their addiction is not a disease. Addicted individuals may realize they are addicted, but they prefer to not seek help, continuing in their addiction instead."[4] In short, every addict is at risk of living in this stage, which is a set-up for failure.

Stages of Relapse

One of the most important lessons for any addict to learn is that relapse is not an event. It is a process. Mistakenly, we tend to point to a specific moment when we acted out and see that as the entire problem—the moment we viewed porn, masturbated, met with another women, or acted out in some other way. What we miss is that no one ever falls; they slide. Every instance of acting out is nothing more than the predictable outcome of recent choices we have made. If we "slip" or "relapse" tomorrow, it will be because of something that happened today, yesterday, or last week.

It is important that we recognize the stages of relapse.

1. Emotional Relapse

This is the earliest stage of relapse. A person may not even be thinking about acting out, but his lack of attention to self-care, his isolation, or his slippage in attending recovery meetings and therapy sessions have set him up for failure.

An emotional relapse may occur when a person remembers his last relapse, does not want to repeat it, and is not thinking about going back. But his emotions and resulting behaviors are chipping away at his sobriety, little by little. The emotional stage of relapse is usually met with denial. "After all," the addict tells himself, "I haven't actually done anything yet." And it's true. But before we act out in our bed, we act out in our head.

There are two ways to pull out before emotional relapse progresses to the next level. One is self-care. I urge clients to eat right, exercise, and connect with God and others. The second goal is to help the person face the calamity they may be facing around the next turn. It is through self-awareness that a prolonged fall may be avoided.

2. Mental Relapse

If left untreated, emotional relapse progresses to mental relapse. This stage is characterized by a tug of war between past habits and the desire to change. Romanticizing past behaviors, hanging out with old friends, lying, and thoughts of physical relapse are dancing in our heads. It is critical to engage specific coping skills before things spin completely out of control.

Signs of mental relapse include cravings, thoughts of past acting out events, and minimizing the consequences of unhealthy behaviors. This leads to bargaining. The addict says, "As long as I don't use porn, it's okay to masturbate." Or, "I will only browse dating sites for ten minutes, and I won't reach out to anyone."

Mental relapse is often called "euphoric recall." This happens when we let fantasy extend into the planning out and imaginative parts of our brains. This can be as stimulating as the physical acting out itself. The dopamine rush kicks in, and it becomes nearly impossible to pull back.

It is important that those early in their recovery recognize that a certain level of fantasy will be present for a period. While we can—and should—learn to cut it off, we must not fall into the ditch of perfection. After a few months of sobriety, addicts generally report an uptick in sexualized dreams. Again, this is normal, and one must not condemn himself for that. The key in the mental relapse phase is not to eliminate all sexualized thoughts, but to minimize and mitigate them.

3. Physical Relapse

At this point, the wheels come off. This final stage of relapse occurs when an individual resumes his addictive behaviors. Some researchers have differentiated a "lapse" (an initial use of porn, for example) from a "relapse" (uncontrolled episodes of acting out). Perhaps you are more familiar with the term "slip," which is synonymous with "lapse."

I prefer to not use terms like "slip" and "lapse" too often. To call a return to one's addictive behavior anything less than a "relapse" may only minimize the behavior in the mind of the addict. Further, he might rationalize his actions so that anything less than his bottom line behavior or event is considered something less than a full relapse. This is dangerous on many levels.

Triggers for Relapse

To avoid relapse, you need to be aware of the cravings and triggers. Cravings are just that: urges to act out. When a craving happens, a good strategy is to talk to your sponsor or a trusted support person immediately. Be honest about what you're feeling, get it all out there, and talk it through. Experts in the addiction field have found that simply talking about cravings can significantly reduce their power.

Triggers are trickier and more subtle than cravings. Dr. Lantie Elisabeth Jorandby, a noted psychiatrist and Chief Medical Officer at a leading recovery center in Jacksonville, Florida, has conducted extensive research on the subject of triggers. Her research confirms that triggers can be difficult to identify, and they don't always follow a predictable pattern.[5] The answer is to remain diligent and to learn general triggers that affect most addicts, as well as those triggers which are unique to your situation.

A couple of simple formulas may help with the more general triggers. For years, addicts have been familiar with H.A.L.T. We tend to act out when we are hungry, angry, lonely, or tired. My research concludes that very few guys really have hunger as a primary trigger. But boredom and stress are generally strong triggers for most of us. So, I have created a new acronym: B.L.A.S.T. We tend to act out when we are bored, lonely, angry, stressed, or tired.

Now, let's dig a little deeper into a few triggers that seem to hit most sex and porn addicts in one way or another.

1. Depression

Depression puts a person at a higher risk for suicide. One study reported by *Psychology Today* found that while those suffering from depression have a much higher rate of suicide than others, that rate jumps by 2.5 times for depressed individuals who are also suffering from addiction.[6]

Symptoms of depression include the following:
a. Hopelessness
b. Low energy
c. Significant appetite fluctuation
d. Guilt
e. Feelings of worthlessness
f. Problems concentrating
g. Anxious feelings
h. Change in sleep patterns
i. Irritability

2. Stress

In a survey which I conducted of 91 men in recovery, I found that stress was the #1 trigger to their acting out. A study conducted in Europe found a circular effect. Stress leads to addiction, and addiction leads to stress.[7] It is imperative that the sex addict find ways to mitigate his stress. This also helps to explain why 37 percent of pastors struggle with pornography, in violation of their moral code. Pastors suffer from more stress than most, with endless tasks, never-ending deadlines, and daily pastoral care situations that confront death, illness, and heartache.

A certain amount of stress is normal and unavoidable. The real threat is not stress, but chronic stress.[8] When you feel an ongoing level of stress that leads to a myriad of sexual fantasies and euphoric recall, you must take action.

3. Exhaustion

Relapse often comes to those who are simply exhausted. When life gets out of balance and we don't practice self-care with great intention, we are at risk. We must watch out for lack of sleep, poor eating habits, and lack of down time. One of the things we suggest to all men in recovery, especially pastors, is to have a monthly Recovery Day. This is a day set apart for self-care, fun, meditation, prayer, hobbies, time alone, and anything that feeds serenity. For me, this often includes things like visiting a car museum, walks on the beach, visiting area small towns, an ice cream parlor, a recovery meeting, and prayer.

4. Isolation

Along with abuse and trauma, isolation tends to be at the root of addiction. This is why we need 12-Step fellowships and other groups. I tell the guys in my Freedom Groups that half the benefit of the group is the workbook and exercises; the other half is just hanging out with other guys. To stay sober, we must connect with others in recovery. Sometimes, playing golf with someone who knows our story is as therapeutic as counseling. We get into trouble when we don't get into anything else. It is critical that we not isolate.

5. Other

The number of triggers that lead to relapse is endless. Because each of us is different, our triggers are different. I often observe men as they share their triggers, and think, "This is unbelievable!" I struggle to relate to some triggers. But my personal triggers might sound crazy to many others. While the list of triggers knows no bounds, the following list might be helpful.[9]

    a. The discomfort of withdrawal symptoms
    b. Unpleasant feelings including hunger, anger, loneliness, and fatigue
    c. Seeing old friends who are still in their addiction
    d. Finding oneself in places associated with one's past acting out behaviors
    e. Overconfidence that everything is under control

Creating a Relapse Prevention Plan

"It is not enough to know that we have lost control; we must also know about the disease of addiction that has caused us to lose control. Furthermore, we must know about the steps necessary for recovery."[10] Similarly, we must know the steps necessary to avoid relapse. You need a plan. It needs to be tailored to you and be ready to implement at the moment you're feeling cravings or triggers. This way, you'll be ready to react more effectively to the relapse threat.

An example of a comprehensive, five-point relapse prevention plan:

1. Go to meetings.

Nothing will do more to position you for long-term recovery than going to meetings. A three-year longitudinal study has found that the combination of individual therapy and a support group (such as 12-Step groups) will best position the addict for success.[11]

There are at least four benefits to joining a group:

a. You learn that you're not alone.
b. You learn what addiction and denial sound like by hearing them in others.
c. You learn what strategies have been successful in recovery.
d. You have a safe place to go where you will not be judged.

A thorough study of 12-Step groups has concluded that there are four components to success in 12-Step work.[12]

a. Attend meetings regularly.
b. Work with a sponsor.
c. Work the Steps.
d. Maintain a goal of total sobriety.

2. Work with a sponsor or mentor.

A sponsor is a person of the same sex who is equipped to lead you through the 12 Steps. Sponsors are not professionals; they simply have more sobriety and experience than those who are new to recovery. A mentor is anyone who is trained in leading a porn or sex addict through the process of recovery. What is most beneficial about this relationship is not the information the sponsor or mentor can offer, but the relationship.

3. Work with a therapist as needed.

We all need to be in therapy from time to time. Try to find a therapist who is familiar with the unique challenges of vocational ministry. For struggles with sex addiction, it is always much better to find a local C.S.A.T.—Certified Sex Addiction Therapist. If you have not completed a full clinical disclosure for your wife, a C.S.A.T. can facilitate that process. It is good to see a qualified therapist from time to time, just to keep your recovery on track.

4. Practice diligent self-care.

It is important to get out of your negative headspace with music, a long walk, or even medication. Schedule monthly Recovery Days. Plan for Recovery Night exercises with your spouse. Be good to yourself. Exercise. Eat right. Get plenty of sleep. Take up a new hobby. Return to an old hobby. Visit a new town. Find a new restaurant. Go for a bike ride. Fly a kite. Call an old friend. Do something for you!

5. Take inventory after every relapse.

Ask yourself what was going on before the relapse that wasn't going on in previous days when there was no relapse. What was going on in your mind and around you for the last 24 hours? The last 24 minutes? The last 24 seconds? Learn to break down the triggers and your response to those triggers. Take note of the things you could have done differently, such as calling a sponsor, practicing the 20-minute rule, or just going for a walk. And always tell someone if there has been a relapse.

Relapse Prevention from Cognitive Behavioral Therapy

One of the therapeutic tools that has been successfully utilized to prevent relapse is known as cognitive behavioral therapy. This specialized approach has been proven to change negative thinking and treat anxiety, depression, and addiction. The basic idea of cognitive therapy is that negative thinking is learned thinking and therefore it can be unlearned and replaced with healthier thinking.[13] If you change your thinking, you will change your life.

Dr. Steven Melemis, expert on addiction and mood disorders, and author of *I Want to Change My Life*, offers four preventative measures from the perspective of cognitive therapy.[14]

1. Fear. A basic fear of recovery is that we will not be capable of successful recovery. Past relapse is seen as proof that we cannot get well. With effective therapy, the client redirects this fear into effective coping skills.
2. Redefining fun. When under stress, a client glamorizes his past. The addiction is seen as fun. Effective therapy redirects this to healthy outlets.
3. Learning from setbacks. Setbacks must be seen as a normal part of progress. Failure is not a setback, but an unwillingness to learn from it.
4. Being comfortable with the uncomfortable. It's okay to wrestle with feelings of fear and defeat. Clients must be led out of the escape to addiction.

The bottom line is that relapse prevention takes work, and a lot of it. Long-term recovery doesn't just happen. Writer and addiction specialist Amy Keller says it like this: "For many, the action required for relapse prevention is both physically and mentally taxing."[15]

Risks for Those with Good Sobriety

The good news is that with longer recovery, the chances for relapse diminish. As the addict builds momentum, reverting to old habits gradually becomes less of a threat.[16] But it is critical to remember that any addiction is a chronic disease. Thus, the threat of relapse is always present. Despite acquiring the skills and tools necessary to avoid relapse, a relapse may still occur. (As of this writing, I know a man who just reset his sobriety date after eight years of sobriety.)

In late-stage recovery, individuals are subject to special risks of relapse that are not often seen in early stages. Clinical experience has shown that the following are some of the causes of relapse in the growth stage of recovery.[17]

Broken Vessels

1. Clients often want to put their addiction behind them and forget they ever had a problem.
2. As life improves, they focus less on self-care.
3. Clients begin to feel they have learned all they need to know.
4. Addicts assume they can move beyond the basics and no longer engage in recovery activities.

Chapter 11
A WORD TO THE CHURCH

The Bible gives a clarion call to the local church. "Dear brothers and sisters, if another believer is overcome by some sin, you who are godly should gently and humbly help that person back onto the right path" (Galatians 6:1). This is the responsibility of the church, whether that "right path" leads the fallen pastor back into public ministry or not.

A failure of character on the part of a pastor or staff member creates a situation for which most churches are not prepared. They endure a crisis of enormous proportion and usually respond on the fly. Unfortunately, few churches are proactive in this area, and therefore have no template for how to respond to these challenging times.

So what's the answer? Both the church and her pastor bear responsibility for creating a pathway forward. The church needs to be a redemptive fellowship that is safe even for her leaders. And the pastor needs to live a confessional life. I like the way Tal Prince says it: "The pastor needs to lead with a limp."[1] Together, the pastor and church can move through just about any difficulty, if they truly seek God's face.

But as we have said, there are situations in which it is nearly impossible for the pastor/church relationship to continue. If the relationship is to be preserved, there is one indispensable element that absolutely must be in place. Without this, there is no hope for restoration.

Repentance

In the online resource, *The Healing of a Warrior*, by Michael L. and Sharon P. Hill, a step-by-step process of identifying real repentance is suggested. If these qualities are not present, there is assuredly a lack of true repentance and any hope for restoration is gone.[2]

1. Confession: sincere regret and an acknowledgment of the magnitude of the sin and why it was wrong.
2. Change of attitude and behavior: a shift from blaming others to a willingness to bear the blame.
3. Following a plan: a willingness to follow a written contract detailing steps for restoration.
4. Accountability: a willingness to meet with one biblically grounded mature believer each week who will prepare a report of the leader's progress

A Spiritual Crisis

While the church must confront the crisis of a pastor's failure, they will also need to address the spiritual crisis that ensues. How much should church leaders tell the congregation? What are the ways in which the church can prepare the way for the church to navigate these suddenly choppy waters? Several principles might be helpful.

1. Tell the church something.

There is nothing worse than a congregation gathering one Sunday only to find their pastor has been dismissed, without any explanation. But many churches proceed this way. The theory is, "What they don't know won't hurt them." Sometimes, church leaders experience paralysis by analysis. They can't find the perfect way to tell the church, so they say nothing. But in the absence of information, the congregation will create their own narrative. Gossip and rumors will ensue. This is never healthy; the church leadership must say something.

Eddie Sharp, senior consultant with the Siburt Institute for Church Ministry at Abilene Christian University in Texas, says,

"The end of a ministry may be legitimate, but that will never make it easy."[3] The issues must be processed and the church must be told.

2. Don't tell the church everything.

The church doesn't need to know every gory detail of every staff dismissal. I love the way Dr. Roger Barrier says it. He offers the following template. When he has had to inform his churches of a pastoral dismissal, he says something like, "I want you to know that X can no longer work in our church. He has done something that violates our trust and compromises his ability to continue in his/her job. I want you to treat him/her and their family with love and grace as we work through this difficult time for both him and the church. I will not tell you what he/she did. But, I want you to remember that there is not one thing he did that many of you haven't done, too."[4]

3. Seek outside counsel.

Every denomination has men and women who are equipped with necessary skills to walk beside churches in crisis. And non-denominational churches usually are joined with like-minded congregations in various networks. Numerous consultants and former pastors have been specifically trained to guide churches through the dismissal process. Dr. Mark Chaves, of Duke University, reports that in a given year, 33 percent of all American churches seek outside counsel, and 40 percent of those involve some sort of staff management issue or crisis.[5]

4. Settle in for a period of transition.

When the church dismisses her pastor, she needs to prepare for a long and winding road ahead. Things will not return to normal soon, if ever. A transition team should be put into place, which will work tirelessly to create a process of healing which lays out initial steps by which the church can move forward. Part of this plan will likely include hiring an interim pastor, holding listening sessions for church members, and gathering for significant hours of prayer.

Observations on Pastoral Firings

As a senior pastor for 31 years, I was always proud of the staff unity we enjoyed in my churches. For the most part, our staff prayed together and we played together. I was careful to involve our spouses as much as possible, usually including them on an annual retreat. In hiring staff, I looked for three things: (a) character, (b) competence, and (c) chemistry. (The one most pastors place too little emphasis on is chemistry.)

I also learned to hire people I already knew, whenever possible. I once read about a megachurch study that said that one in two hirings don't work out well, unless a prior relationship is already established; whereas, when the pastor already knows the new staff person, the success rate jumps to 80 percent.

Here are a few things I learned through the years.

1. Don't hire someone you can't afford to fire.

A deacon told me this one time. I was considering hiring a young man as our Student Pastor, who had grown up in that church, and whose family were key leaders in the church. He was a rising star, so I pushed him through the hiring process. Sure enough, things went poorly, we had to dismiss him, and it cost me some dear friends.

2. When you need to fire someone, get it over with.

I don't think I ever dismissed a man too soon. Many times, I did it too late. When it becomes obvious that a change needs to be made, there is no use in waiting. Any delay will only make things worse.

3. No one ever thinks they deserve to be fired.

In even the most obvious firings, the person who is dismissed will protest the decision. The senior leadership of the church needs to know this going in. A dismissal cannot become a negotiation. The leadership must be sure of its decision; then proceed.

4. Every staff person has supporters.

I learned that the best pastor has detractors and the worst pastor has supporters. Know that any staff change will be met with resistance from some corners of the church. If you are in position to dismiss a staff person, just know that this decision will not be met with unanimous support.

5. There is no good way to let someone go.

Letting a staff person go is never easy. While there are some ways that are worse than others, none is much fun. This is especially true when letting a senior pastor go. Expect turmoil and false accusations, no matter how well it may be handled.

6. When you dismiss someone, they will never like you again.

It is natural to want to go back and rebuild broken relationships with ministers who have been dismissed from the church. But with rare (very rare) exceptions, know that this is not going to happen. Nothing short of a miracle of God's grace and healing will pave the way for healthy reconciliation.

How Should the Church Respond?

Again, very few churches have a plan in place. The result is that they must deal with the most traumatic crisis imaginable with zero planning. That is a huge mistake. The best response is preemptive, meaning it is wise to create the boundaries and redemptive culture that will best protect both the pastor and the church. Then it is critical to remember the issue is not *if* your pastor struggles with porn, but *when*. Since roughly one half of all ministers share this struggle, your church likely has a minister on staff who is struggling with porn *right now*. Let's assume two things happen. First, your pastor is struggling or has struggled with porn or sex addiction. Second, this has been discovered. Now what do you do as a church? We suggest several guiding principles.

1. Think redemptively.

This does not mean that every pastor should keep his position in the church after he is discovered. But the fundamental principle that should guide *every response* to a pastor's fall, no matter how egregious, is redemption. You may not redeem his position, but that should never be the primary goal anyway. It is about redeeming the man. Perhaps it will help if you remember his problem is one of the head and not the heart. I've never heard of a pastor who wants to be a sex addict. They feel more shame than any other addict—more than you can imagine. Jesus said, "A battered reed he [God] will not break off, and a smoldering wick he will not put out" (Matthew 12:20). In other words, God still has a plan for the fallen pastor. There is nothing he could ever do to make God love him more, and nothing he has ever done has made God love him less.

As for redeeming a fallen pastor to the pastoral ministry again, I agree with Jared Wilson: "Grace either covers all sin repented of, or it covers none."[6] This is not to say every pastor can be returned to vocational ministry, but that we must be at least open to that possibility.

John Piper expounds on this. "Is it possible to restore a pastor who sinned sexually but who is repentant? Or is such a pastor disqualified because he no longer meets the qualification of being 'above reproach'? I'm afraid if I answer this the way that I should, it will give so much license to restore pastors too quickly. But since I should, I should. Ultimately, I think the answer is yes. A pastor who has sinned sexually can be a pastor again. And I say that just because of the grace of God and the fact that 'above reproach' can be restored."[7]

2. Respond biblically.

It is a grave mistake to respond to a pastor's failings as though we didn't have a Bible to guide us. The church is unlike any other institution in the world. The Bible is our handbook. So when you respond to a pastor's sin, consult the handbook. (Better yet, have a biblical plan already in place.) There are several Scriptures you need to wrestle with. The pastor is to be "above reproach" (1 Timothy 3:2). The Bible also says, "There is forgiveness with God" (Psalm 130:4). The question of whether a pastor can be returned to his position following his discovery is informed by many factors: whether he was already in recovery when he was discovered, whether he had an affair with someone in the church, whether he used church funds to pay for his habit, and whether he is truly repentant and willing to go to any length to get well. Each church must answer these questions based on its own heritage and interpretation of the Scriptures.

3. React compassionately.

Sadly, when most pastors fall, they are confronted by a few men in the church, forced to resign, instructed to not return to the church, and then completely abandoned. They are written out of the church history, treated as though their tenure at the church (and all the good things they achieved) never happened, and kicked to the curb. The church ends all contact with them, apart from a small severance.

Remember, church, the world is your audience. They are watching you! There are a few examples of churches where the pastor was discovered in the height of his addiction, and properly removed from his position, but with time was restored to the fellowship, if not his position. The church walked with him—and his family—through their darkest valley.

Church—do not abandon your pastor *or his wife*! They suddenly have no job, probably have to move, and are scared. While it is true that his sin has found him out (Numbers 32:23), grace needs to find him as well. So when you react to your pastor's fall, keep a few things in mind. Remember how Jesus dealt with the woman caught in adultery—and with her accusers. Remember that the same Peter who denied even knowing Jesus was sent out just a few weeks later to preach the most important sermon in the history of Christianity.

Ethicist and seminary professor Dr. Miroslav Kis writes, "In ministering to the fallen pastor, the church ministers to her own wounds, as well."[8] By reacting compassionately, the church blesses the pastor, his family, and the entire congregation.

4. Provide financially.

Your pastor now needs a job. He will likely need to move. This means his wife, if she is working outside the home, will need to find a new job, as well. They need counseling. Additionally, they are in the most shame-filled, desperate moments of their lives. Never is a man more vulnerable, even suicidal, than when he is brought to public shame because of a porn or sex addiction. This is not to excuse him—at all. But if the church is to be the body of Christ, she will not shoot her wounded. I suggest, whether your pastor—or any other staff member who falls—has been at your church for one year or twenty years, give him a minimum of six months' severance pay when he is dismissed. Make it a full year if at all possible. He needs time for personal recovery and restoration and to find his way forward with his calling and career. Forcing him to figure it all out with just one or two months of pay is brutal. In his darkest hour your pastor doesn't need justice—he needs mercy.

Jim Meyer, writing for Restoring Kingdom Builders, offers several suggestions as to why a terminated pastor should receive a severance package. Some of these reasons follow.[9]

   a. It usually takes a pastor at least a year to find another ministry. Because there are fewer church openings than ever today, finding a ministry job *is* a job. A severance package allows the pastor to pursue his divine calling, which is why some denominations, such as the Lutheran Missouri Synod have passed resolutions that direct member churches to give forced-out pastors a severance of one full year's salary.
   b. Most pastors lack the required training and skills to land a secular job that pays them a livable wage. Many secular jobs require a lengthy certification process—including further education, which costs money—and even if a pastor completes the requirements, there is no guarantee that anyone will hire him. In addition, many secular employers are fearful that an ex-pastor may spend his time trying to convert fellow employees to his faith, rather than concentrating on his job. Because of their divine

call to ministry, pastors are often unsuited for other professions.
c. Since pastors do not pay into unemployment, they are not eligible to receive it. A severance package—which includes salary plus medical insurance—provides the pastor the best possible bridge to his next position.
d. After a pastor resigns, he still has to meet his financial obligations. He has to pay his mortgage, property taxes, and utilities; car payments and auto insurance; food and gasoline bills; and medical insurance for his family, among other payments. When church leaders want a pastor to resign, but are unwilling to give him a severance agreement, the leaders seem to be engaging in retribution rather than reconciliation.
e. The terminated pastor usually has to rebuild his life and ministry, and that takes anywhere from one to three years. When pastors leave a church abruptly, it devastates them mentally, emotionally, physically, and spiritually, often sending them into deep depression. A severance package allows the pastor to pull away from ministry and promotes the healing process.
f. The world is watching to see how the church will treat her fallen pastor. This includes young men and women considering a life in ministry, new believers, unbelievers, and the pastor's supporters.

Each church will review her situation differently, depending on the pastor's mistakes, tenure, and the traditions of the church. Our recommendation is that any church is wise to err on the side of generosity. Keeping in mind that any severance pay benefits the pastor's family, and not just the pastor himself, the church that provides abundantly mirrors the grace of the Gospel. For that reason, we suggest that the church provide a minimum of six months' severance.

5. Plan proactively.

We have already said this. Have a plan in place before you need it. Assume that you will need to address this kind of issue at some point. If you prepare your buildings for the 0.7 percent who will need a wheelchair ramp, you should prepare your processes for the 50 percent of pastors who struggle with porn. David L. Bea, attorney for churches, writes, "It is prudent for churches to periodically review their policies and procedures with qualified legal counsel."[10]

6. Proceed courageously.

Karl Vaters, with Innovative Ministry, is right: "Leading a church is often a lesson in managing and overcoming frustration."[11] Indeed, nothing is more frustrating for a church than dealing with a problem they did not create—the moral failure of her pastor. But this is a great chance to rise up as the children of God.

Think big! What would it say to the world if you didn't fire your pastor? What if you put together a two-year plan by which he could return to his position, having concluded necessary counseling and treatment under careful supervision? Or if you feel he has disqualified himself from serving in this capacity and simply cannot remain in—or return to—his staff position, what if you brought him back to the church at a future point for the purpose of reconciliation and celebration? What if he completes successful therapy and finds lasting recovery, and you bring him in for a special occasion so he and his wife can share their story, make public amends, and receive the prayers and support of the church they served? What if the community saw you reconciling with your pastor in a way that was restorative and redemptive?

This takes courage. Any church can take their pastor's picture off the wall, remove him from the history books, and pretend he never existed. But is that what Jesus would do? At some point, one of your pastors or staff leaders will fall. Be ready. And when he or she does, *think redemptively, respond biblically, react compassionately, provide financially, plan proactively, and proceed courageously!*

Chapter 12
OUR STORIES

God uses broken people. In fact, *God only uses broken people.* Why? Because there are no other kind. But I know what you are thinking—there is broken, and then there is broken. And any minister of the Gospel who has fallen into sexual sin is *broken*.

Diane Shirlaw-Ferreira wrote a helpful article, "God Uses Broken People—4 Reasons God Uses the Weak to Do Amazing Things." She writes, "Let's face it. Most of God's disciples could have been residents on the Island of the Misfit Toys! No one is too broken for God. We all have broken pieces and God uses all our broken pieces and puts them together again in ways only he could and he solidifies them in his refining fire and molds us into what he knows we can be."[1]

Behind every success story is a personal connection. I say it a lot: the opposite of addiction is not recovery; it is community. It is through personal connections that we find lasting recovery. That is one reason I am not reluctant to tell my own story. When I was "discovered," and eventually followed God's call to launch a recovery ministry, many well-meaning friends offered the same advice. "Don't tell your story." That may work for some, but for me it doesn't. Of course, there is a balance here. My story doesn't bring recovery to anyone, including me. Recovery comes from following specific steps. But we identify with stories.

The reason I continue to attend a weekly 12-Step meeting (SA) isn't that I am in search for that one piece of information that I somehow missed in the first 800 meetings I attended (as of this writing). It's all about connection.

Addiction cripples, but secrets kill. For pastors, this presents a tremendous challenge. If you admit to those around you, "I am a plumber and I am a sex addict," you will not likely lose your job. But say, "I am a pastor and I am a sex addict," and you will likely lose your job, ministry, reputation, denominational credentials, and quite a few friends. You may need to move your family across the country and start a whole new life.

I know that because it happened to me. One day, I was the senior pastor of a thriving church with over 2,000 members. Within three months after my "discovery," I had moved from Texas to Florida, was driving for Uber, delivering groceries, and creating a new circle of friends.

What saved me was the personal connections I have made through these years of recovery.

Along this journey, I have met dozens of pastors who share my struggle. Some remain in their ministry positions, while many do not. Each is an inspiration, for they are in the battle. I count many of them among my closest friends. And because I know we find strength from the stories of others, I have asked some of them to share theirs. What you are about to read are the stories of some of the bravest men I know. Some of these ministers are very well known, while others are not. But don't try to identify them. I have scrambled a few of the non-essential details in order to protect their anonymity, and have not used their real names.

My prayer is that you will find yourself in some of these stories, that through them you might find strength. These men come from various denominational backgrounds, though all are Christian. They represent different types of ministries and come from several continents. They share two things in common—their love for Jesus and their commitment to recovery.

Frank

I grew up as a preacher's kid, so faith and religion permeated my world like oxygen. As the oldest of four boys, the blessing of a pastor's home soon became like a curse. I took on the role of the "perfect child." I failed to live up to the pressure. As I struggled to deal with these unstated expectations that I heaped on myself, I sought a way of escape from the waves of feelings and emotions that filled my heart and mind.

As a boy of around ten, I discovered masturbation. Around the same time, a neighbor friend covertly showed me his father's stash of pornography magazines. Even though we only gawked at the pictures for a moment, the images burned their way into my mind. I could recall them in vivid detail simply by closing my eyes. Soon, I imagined what other girls and women would look like beneath their clothes. These "lust hits" fueled my masturbation as I sought to escape from the pressure to measure up.

One day, to my horror, my mother walked in on me. Unprepared for what she saw, she disciplined me. She ordered me to stop. My dad never said a word to me. Later she tried to reverse course by telling me that it was normal for boys to explore their bodies and physical drives. The conflicting messages did nothing but drive me deeper into a secret world. I learned to sneak around and hide my actions. Guilt and shame became constant companions. I numbed these negative emotions with my drug of choice—lust and masturbation.

Amid these struggles in my secret life, God called me to be a pastor. His call confused me. The joy of his call thrilled my heart. I surrendered to his call. I fought my secret obsession with prayer, confession, pleas for healing, even at one desperate moment anointing myself for healing.

Over time I became very accustomed to living a double life. My ministry to God became my amends for my secret struggles. My self-deception reached the point that I allowed myself to act out on certain days and not others. I lied to myself and others.

In 1995, we had our first internet account. Suddenly, in secret, I explored internet pornography. The dark world of online pornography sucked me in. Cravings for more and more stirred. I longed for secret moments alone so I could gorge myself on the images.

God offered me an opportunity to escape the first time my wife walked in on me. A flash of shame struck my heart and soul. Excuses and justifications poured out of my mouth. As an act of penance, I sought out counseling. I sobered up for a season, only to return to my double life. A few years later, my wife caught me. I looked up the location of a local Sexaholics Anonymous (SA) group. Afraid of exposure, I never acted on my good instinct to get help.

Fast forward twenty years, and still trapped in a double life, my computer screen told the truth about my compulsive behavior. This time my wife placed the open laptop in front of me and walked out of the room. Suddenly, I found myself alone in a silent room. I wondered if she had given up on me.

That day my journey toward wholeness and sanity began. Once again, I looked up a local SA group. This time I called. I asked for help. The next day I walked into my first face-to-face SA meeting. Not knowing what to expect, I entered a room to be welcomed by a solitary figure. That day, God had arranged for me to have a one-on-one encounter with another man who knew my struggles. He shared his story, which sounded so much like my story. That room became a "thin place" for me—a place where heaven and earth touched. No longer did I walk alone.

Recovery and authentic relationships go hand in hand for me. Isolation and lies lead only to trouble defined by a double life. Daily progress—one day at a time—-maps success for me now. Capturing my thoughts and surrendering them to God has replaced my "white knuckle" attempts to stop my acting out. To this day, I thank God for bringing me to the end of myself. Now I know I cannot change, but God can change me. Every day I determine to let him, with the help of others who share the journey with me.

Hector

I grew up singing the children's chorus,

Running over, running over,
My cup is full and running over.
Since the Lord saved me
I'm as happy as can be
.My cup is full and running over.

Broken Vessels

I was a happy child, anxious to please my parents, who were strict disciplinarians. My parents believed, "Spare the rod and spoil the child." Sunday School and Sunday morning and evening church attendance were required. I enjoyed going to church because most of my extended family attended the same church.

At the age of seven, my Sunday School teacher explained the plan of salvation to me in Sunday School class. I was excited to accept God into my heart and life. I was guilty of the normal seven-year-old sins and was thrilled to know God personally and to have God, who loved me, living in my heart. God was going to help me live a life that was pleasing to him and my strict, disciplinarian parents.

My life changed when I was nine years old. Over a period of two years, I was molested by a close relative. I knew that what he did to me and what he made me do to him were wrong. I had read the Old Testament accounts of Sodom and Gomorrah. I questioned to myself, "What did I do or say to make my abuser think that I liked doing such things?" I didn't go to my parents about what was happening for fear of being severely punished. I didn't go to anyone at church because I was afraid I would be judged and labeled a sinner. I didn't go to the police because I thought I would be arrested. I was conflicted because, as bad as I knew the acts were, some of the acts did "feel good."

I lived in two worlds. In one world I was acting like a happy adolescent, while in the second world I was filled with shame, guilt, and self-loathing, craving more attention and affection, wanting to "feel good." Feeling good helped to numb my shame, guilt, and self-loathing. Over time, little by little, I was consumed more and more by my emotions, my feelings, and the sexual acts that continued from my adolescence.

I lived the double life from my adolescence into my adult years. I prayed over and over that God would take away my negative feelings and the sexual desires that consumed and controlled me. I prayed for strength to stop acting out. I prayed for God to give me whatever it took for me to be the Christian that he wanted me to be. I felt like my prayers went no further than the top of my head.

Broken Vessels

My unanswered prayers and my inability to stop acting out confirmed I was a terrible person and a weak Christian. Nothing brought relief or help. As a pastor of 30 years, I was powerless over my compulsive sexual behavior. I had become very adept at living in two worlds. On the occasions when I was questioned about any unusual behavior or strange meetings I was able to lie my way through. I had become a convincing, believable liar.

The cup of my adolescence that once overflowed with joy and happiness was now broken. My little cup now had cracks and holes and oozed a dark, stinking mess of shame, guilt, frustration, anger, and disappointment.

The day my world imploded, a person with whom I was chatting threatened to expose me to my church, my family, and my friends, unless I met his demands. Rather than giving in to his demands I called my wife and my church leadership and confessed my current situation and my need for help with my compulsive sexual behavior.

My wife and my church supported me in my desire to be healthy, whole and holy. My church helped me connect with a therapist who diagnosed me as a sex addict. With my therapist's help, I found and attended my first Sexaholics Anonymous 12-Step group. At that first meeting I got a sponsor who agreed to walk with me on my journey to sexual sobriety and recovery. I left that SA meeting believing my life was not hopeless. In the days and months following, as I have worked the steps with my sponsor, I have come to enjoy a relationship with God that is richer, fuller, and deeper than I have ever known.

For the first time in more than 55 years, I can sing again the chorus of my youth and know the words are true in my heart. My little cup that for decades was cracked and broken has been mended by the Master Potter. I am now a broken, mended vessel loved and being used by God.

Jim

My grandfather was a pastor. My dad was a pastor. My roots in the church were firmly entrenched. If the church was open for a worship service, Bible study, business meeting, or choir rehearsal, we were there. If the church was closed but someone needed to vacuum the carpet, mop the floors, print and fold the weekly programs, straighten the Bibles and hymnals in the back of the pews, or fill the communion trays with those tiny plastic cups, we were there. As a child and deep into my twenties, every single major event in my life was celebrated at church with our church family or not at all. My faith life was on autopilot from the time I was born until I got to college and ran into a group of believers who were passionate about Christ and the Word of God in a way that I found refreshing. Their love for Christ drew me in and brought the Scriptures that I'd always read and recited to life. Their enthusiasm for the things of God rubbed off on me, and the faith that I'd always professed moved from just my head down into my heart. Shortly after that I began teaching and eventually preaching the Word of God at my own church and at various conferences, workshops, retreats, camps, and services around the country.

Before I learned how to write my name in cursive, I had already viewed pornographic magazines. By the time I played in my first Little League Baseball game, I had been sexually abused by a teenage girl who was a distant cousin. Before I was allowed to watch R-rated movies, I had already been tricked into entering the bedroom of a teenage boy in my neighborhood who sexually abused me and a close friend. Not surprisingly, porn and masturbation became close friends and comforters in my adolescence and early adulthood.

Shortly after getting my first job, I started noticing signs that said, "Adult Movies" and "Adult Modeling Studio." While I wasn't actually sure what those words meant, I was curious and quickly found out what the "Adult" in "Adult Movie" meant. Within a few weeks after noticing the signs, I started visiting these businesses. At first, I told myself I was just going to look. There was a definite high that came from just the thought of visiting those places and a rush of energy and excitement that shot through me when I did enter and look around. Eventually, I did more than just look. I crossed all of the boundaries in those places that I said I would never cross. I preached my first sermon before I visited my first adult massage parlor. I hired my first prostitute before I got engaged. I purchased my first pornographic DVD before I purchased my first DVD player or rented my first apartment to put it in.

I told myself that I would stop. Every time was the last time, until it wasn't. Then I got married. I promised myself that I would never do it again. I told myself that my commitment to God and my wife would be enough to keep me from going back to my acting out behaviors. I was wrong. Even on my honeymoon, I was looking for other opportunities to feed my addiction. Then my wife confronted me about a name that appeared in my internet search history. In frustration, I shouted, "What do you want from me?"

She shouted, "I want the truth!"

"The truth?" I thought. Why not a new car, a bigger apartment, a house, a divorce, or my right arm? Why the truth? I couldn't shake the request. A few weeks later, I sat her down and told her why I couldn't pay my bills when we were engaged, why I didn't save up for the honeymoon, why I kept getting overdraft charges, and why I kept making withdrawals from seemingly random ATMs that charged $5.00 to $10.00 to access my own cash.

We reached out for help. A church mentor recommended a C.S.A.T. who happened to have an opening that same week. I dove into individual and group therapy, began attending 12-Step meetings two to three times a week, did daily intimacy exercises with my wife, weekly check-ins with my sponsor, therapist, and my wife, and other daily and weekly program activities. With all of these supports in place, I was able to stop the compulsive behavior and I've seen the urges and compulsions subside greatly over time. It's been years since I've visited an "Adult" business or website. I tried to stop on my own and failed for years. When I confessed and got help, God provided me with a rich network of support. I finally gained traction and found freedom.

Eduardo

I did not grow up with a good role model for sexual integrity. My father had porn in the house, told lewd stories, and had an objectified view of women. He was not kind to my mother, other than being a provider. I was exposed to porn as a child, sexually abused once by an older boy, and began masturbation as a young teenager.

I was saved at age 17 and Jesus began to change me in many ways, but I never made him Lord over my sin of lust. It followed me into marriage and ministry and I was not a good husband. My lusting eventually developed into a full-blown addiction to pornography and masturbation while serving as a senior pastor. I lived a double life until I was caught watching a video in my office at age 62. As a result, I was forced to "retire" early after nearly 38 years of ministry. My wife of over 42 years was totally shocked and devastated, to say the least. She is suffering from the shock and trauma of learning that her "pure-hearted, godly husband" was not so pure-hearted and not so godly. The trauma of my betrayal has been devastating to her and our marriage.

I tried to begin recovery right away, but I was totally ignorant of any of the basics of recovery. I lied to the deacons and my wife, telling them that when I was caught, it was a "one-time event" when I made a "bad judgment call" by "clicking on a pop-up." I also told them that I was not addicted and that was not who I was. My disclosure to my wife was staggered and prolonged over months, as I slowly admitted and revealed more to her, which traumatized her all the more.

Although by God's grace, I was able to stop porn use and masturbation right away, I continued edging behavior with social media for a while, having compartmentalized that as "non-porn." My wife discovered my social media history and confronted me. I immediately stopped viewing social media and devices of any kind unless my wife was right there with me. In my recovery of over four and a half years, I have struggled with keeping promises, lying, fantasy, and other issues related to my thought life and seeing women in public. My wife is still with me, but I have a long way to go to rebuild her trust.

My recovery efforts have included seeing a C.S.A.T. therapist, participating in five weekly online recovery groups, daily calls with an accountability partner, weekly calls with my son, reading books on recovery and spiritual growth, regular physical exercise, online recovery courses, accountability software on all devices, daily disciplines of Bible study, prayer, journaling, Bible reading, meditation, and nightly text reports to one of my groups. Recovery related discussions with my wife have also been extremely helpful, though painful.

One of the greatest helps in my recovery has been my morning Bible study, journaling, and prayer time. While serving as a pastor, my Bible study time usually focused on looking for good sermon topics. In my retirement, I have been doing Bible study the way it should have always been—reading the Bible to discover what God is saying to me to change my life!

I am working to fully recover and to rebuild trust with my wife. My goal is for us to experience emotional intimacy in marriage the way it should have always been and that, together, we can help others who are struggling with sexual addiction and trauma.

I will suffer the consequences of my sin for the rest of my life. But the story does not end there. In keeping with Romans 8:28, I believe God has plans to use my sin for his glory. He has already used my recovery time to draw me closer to him than ever before. He is using me to encourage other men who struggle. I want to be used by God to help more men find freedom from pornography and sexual sin. I also want to sound the alarm about the dangers and the extreme consequences of pornography in every area of life and society.

My hope is not in myself, my wife, my marriage, my counselor, my accountability partner, or my accountability groups. My hope is in Jesus! I am relying upon his forgiveness, grace, mercy and the promises of his Word. 2 Peter 1:3 says, "His divine power has given us everything we need for life and godliness." I find hope in the words of Jesus when he said in John 8:38, "If the Son sets you free, you will be free indeed."

Jacob

I don't remember a time when faith and church weren't a part of my life. Church was certainly the biggest part of my life growing up. There was no choice; if something was happening at church, I was there. I really didn't mind it, even into my adolescent years, because it was my safe place; it was where I fit. If you asked me when I got "saved," I would take you back to the time when I watched my sister, in a drama presentation, get dragged to hell.

Over time, there were more moments and encounters with God. A lot of those moments would happen at places like youth camp, where I felt God calling me to ministry early in my high school career. I didn't know what the path to ministry would look like, but everyone around me seemed to agree and push me toward a life in ministry. As I went to college, I was able to pursue my degree to specifically go into ministry and was able to get a position at a church before I graduated from college. What appeared to be going well wasn't and two weeks before my wedding my world came crashing down. The build-up to this moment was years in the making and would sadly continue for years afterward. A hidden and secret life that I thought was safe and out of view was destroying me in many ways. A close call wasn't enough to stop my addiction. It helped me to feel invincible and safe, no matter how out of control I truly was.

Secrecy and hiddenness were vital parts of my life. At the beginning of middle school, I was introduced to pornography by my father. For my entire middle school life, he would use pornography to sexually abuse me. When the abuse stopped with him, a youth volunteer from church picked up right where he left off. All told, about five years of sexual abuse left me in a lonely and horrible place. I was an addict. Pornography had taken a hold of my life and for a total of 23 years it would completely consume and destroy me from the inside out. Every time I thought I could stop, I couldn't, and my addiction would get worse. I thought going to a Christian university would change everything, but it didn't. I thought getting a job as a pastor would change me for good, but it didn't. I just knew getting married would fix all my issues, but it didn't. The shame and guilt built up over time to where I grew numb and cold to any connection with anyone and settled in to have a secret and hidden life—a life that was miserable, lonely, and scary.

Twelve years into my marriage, the truth finally came out. Sure, there were other times of discovery and repentance and promises of change, but this time was different. This truly was the bottom. I knew I couldn't go on anymore. I was going to lose everything if I didn't give up my addiction. Within a week of being discovered I was at a treatment facility for addiction. I'll never forget sitting in my room the first couple of nights and thinking, how did I get here? I had left everything behind in a desperate attempt to save my life, my marriage, my family, and my ministry. In that time, it became clear that God was after me. It wasn't about my marriage being saved, my ministry being restored, or my reputation being spared. God had a healing planned for my life.

Pain, fear, and anger that had been building for years, finally would be dealt with. I spent 12 weeks diving into the why of my addiction. It seemed obvious where my issues began, but why was I trapped and how could I be set free? It truthfully started with Jesus, and recognizing that his love and value for me didn't come from being a pastor. I became convinced that even as messed up as I was, Jesus still loved me. My addiction ended up costing me a lot, literally and figuratively. I still have many regrets and the pain still feels so fresh at times, but I no longer walk in shame. I never want to be at the place I was before, believing lies and almost losing all that mattered to me. God has been so gracious to me and has surrounded me with amazing support. As everything has unfolded, for the first time in my life I have experienced God's grace tangibly. When anger and judgment should have been thrown my way, I was given mercy and grace. God has reminded me throughout this process of recovery that he hasn't left me or forgotten me. He still has a plan for me and there is hope. My story is far from over and it's not one to be ashamed of. It's a beautiful picture and story of the goodness and the grace of God that is available to all who call on him.

Thomas

I became a Christian when I was five. My dad pastored in my younger years and he did a good job of introducing me to

Jesus. I had no idea how merciful God's timing was. My mother left my father shortly thereafter and I was exposed to much, but God's hand was always with me. I loved the Lord my whole life. And he has loved me! The older I got, the more I understood that holiness was the key to happiness. I sought the Lord in his presence consistently and he never failed to draw me closer and closer.

He called me into his service while I was in college. He has consistently taught me about the power of intimacy with him (John 17:3) and wowed me with his deep thoughts (1 Corinthians 2:10). I'm as excited to be in the Lord today as I ever was!

I spent years battling with pornography. Within a year of becoming a believer, my mother left my father and took me with her to live in a house where my older cousins introduced me to pornography. I was six. I was allowed to stay up late with them watching late-night cable TV. My cousins would channel surf looking for anything sexual on the movie channels. Not long after that, my older cousins got bold and started stealing our grandfather's pornographic magazines that he kept under his bed. That was, until my grandfather found out and secretly threatened them to stop. Nonetheless, what my older cousins had they shared with me. At the age of six I believed that this was simply what boys did.

At age 11, my battle was solidified. My mother's boyfriend moved in with us. He would rent hardcore pornographic videos from the movie rental store and allow me to watch them with him with my mother's permission. Yes, that should make anyone vomit. Sometimes I pray for him. Sometimes I pray against him. The same is true for my mom, I guess. And there was my battle.

Recovery has been sweet to me! The older I've become, the more I've understood that holiness is the key to happiness. I seek the Lord in his presence consistently and he never fails to draw me closer and closer.

I think of all the conversations I had with my pastors over the years, and how those conversations failed to produce holiness in me. It was never easy for outsiders to speak into my situation. They knew the strength of my faith and it left them puzzled and only seeking to encourage me.

What a lie it all was: the pornography cycle that I got caught up in. I thought it had more power than it did. I had trained myself to renew my mind to it to the point that even when I thought I was fighting against it, I was just renewing my mind to it from a distance, so it always made its way back.

When I received the tools to break the cycle of renewing my mind to pornography, everything changed. It took a little bit of time (not much), but I was able to learn new brain pathways so that the things that used to trigger me became laughable. I use the word laughable because I finally figured out how God works through our thinking and his joy has risen up on the inside of me!

Once I broke free from the cycle, I was able to meditate on Romans 6-8, disassociating my thought life in Christ from the old man and his deeds. I was never able to get this far before because I was caught up responding to trigger after trigger. Before this, it didn't matter what I believed. If Satan saw me getting too holy, he could use someone else to trigger me into my learned behavior. But when I was anointed and healed from the cycle of being triggered, I was allowed to be the man whose "delight is in the law of the Lord, And in his law he meditates day and night. He shall be like a tree planted by the rivers of water, that brings forth its fruit in its season, whose leaf also shall not wither; and whatever he does shall prosper."

Simon

I was introduced to pornography at age five when a magazine blew across my front lawn. I was innocently playing when I picked it up and saw a picture of naked bodies mixed together in a way I didn't understand. Even at that young age, something stirred inside of me knowing it was foreign and not right.

Two years later, I had a similar experience, accidentally stumbling across a centerfold. This time I brought it to my parents, hoping they would offer an explanation for the images I didn't understand. But instead of explaining it and warning against it, they simply told me to throw it away. Like many parents, they didn't know how to handle that conversation, so they decided to say nothing at all.

As an adolescent, pornography became readily available through friends and their "dad's stash." Somewhere in middle school I learned to mix the rush of emotions I got from viewing these images with masturbation, and I was hooked. Just as Proverbs 7:22 states, I was like "a deer stepping into a noose." Throughout middle and high school my addiction to pornography was full blown.

It wasn't until college that I realized there was a way out. For me, college was a time of spiritual awakening. I had grown up in the church with head knowledge of who Jesus was and what he had done for me, but was lacking a relationship with him. My freshman year, though, as I began reading the Bible and praying to him, God began making himself real to me in personal ways.

Bible passages were suddenly speaking directly to me and God was answering specific prayers in my life. I was growing spiritually and soon realized some foundational truths. My life was not my own and God had a purpose for me. That purpose started with repentance, and the Holy Spirit put the spotlight on my porn addiction. I willingly confessed my sin because I was eager to break the habit.

As any addict knows, though, simply confessing sin in an area steeped in addiction takes more than just repentance. It requires help from others. Thankfully the Lord put two guys in my life who became my accountability partners. I soon began the slow and arduous process of recovery.

For the next 20 years I tried to be honest with myself, my wife, and the guys that held me accountable. I did experience stints of sobriety, but the urge for pornography kept reining me back into its grip. Relapse was never that far away from me.

I once heard a pastor say that you cannot find healing from your sin until you truly hate your sin. That proved to be true in my life. For years, I fought denial that my struggle "wasn't that bad." I held onto pornography for way too long simply because I didn't hate it enough.

Hating sin means jumping through whatever hoops are necessary, and submitting to whatever authority you need to, in order to break the chains that have held you captive. But for most guys this doesn't happen until their sin truly costs them something.

For me, my addiction finally cost me my job. I had been in various pastoral roles for over 20 years and had just started a new role at a new church. Knowing I needed accountability, I confessed my struggle to the lead pastor. In a deeply painful fashion, this pastor exposed my struggles to the church body and asked for my resignation. It was shocking and humiliating and caused me to hit rock bottom. It also pushed me to be willing to do whatever was necessary in order to change. I now hated my sin.

It was at this point that I met Mark Denison. He helped me walk through my first 90 days of recovery with personal coaching. I started attending SA meetings and checking in with my wife and accountability partners. I became real with God, myself, and others. I held nothing back. Ninety days turned into six months and six months turned into a year. I retrained my brain and learned to deal with stress, loneliness, and boredom in constructive ways. I took it one day at a time, but as the days began to add up, the daily struggle began to go down.

I recently celebrated two years of sobriety from porn and masturbation. Though sobriety is a current reality for me, I know I am always one step away from making a poor choice and reverting back to where I started. Sobriety is a choice I will have to make every day for the rest of my life. But I am living proof that freedom is attainable if you truly hate your sin and are willing to do whatever it takes to eradicate it.

Aasir

2:21 AM! The memory is still so vivid and clear, even though it has been almost two years since that fateful night. I felt my wife crawl into our bed and wondered why she was so late coming to bed. I reached over to touch her and felt her body stiffen. I asked, "Are you OK?" and her reply sent chills down my spine—"NO! I know everything!" As she exited our bed, I reached for my phone, which was typically on my bedside table. Her next words clearly explained why she had come to bed so late—"It's not there!" My wife of 29 years had gone through my phone while I slept and discovered the proof of my affair—something she had suspected for several weeks. Her discovery began the most painful, gut-wrenching, heart-rending, devastating, yet enlightening, exciting, hope-filled journey of my life!

My story actually began many years before this night. My parents were determined to raise my sisters and me in a Christian home, which meant consistent church attendance and strict rules for behavior enforced by heavy discipline. Though I didn't consider myself particularly rebellious, I began, at an early age, deciding which rules I would follow or not follow, earning me the labels, "trouble-maker" and "black-sheep." I was a good student in school and a better athlete. As with many young boys, I had a dream to play college football but I also had the drive and the backing of my coaches to make it happen. All of this changed when I was involved in a car accident that put me in the hospital for three months and in recovery for over a year. My dreams were shattered—I would never again be the same athlete. For the first time, I recall hearing this voice inside of me say, "You are not enough! You don't measure up!" Over time, this voice would grow stronger, along with the sense of rejection and insecurity that accompanied it. As these feelings intensified, my focus shifted toward finding ways to escape the pain—girls, sex, porn, and masturbation were at the top of the list. As a result, I learned how to masturbate at a prepubescent age, lost my virginity when I was 13, and was clueless about how these decisions would eventually impact my life.

At the age of 19, I embraced the realization that I needed a Savior and surrendered my heart and life to Jesus Christ. One year later, I sensed that God was calling me into full-time vocational ministry and said yes to that calling. Both of these decisions came from a desire to follow God in obedience. However, I must admit that I also believed these decisions might reduce, if not completely abolish, the appetite I had created for approval and acceptance. This was not the case! Though I experienced periodic victories, it seemed the slightest thing could send me on a hunt for validation and quite often, I sought the validation from women. The knowledge of women finding me attractive had the ability to fill my "affirmation tank"—at least temporarily. After dating several girls and sleeping with many of them, I finally met THE ONE in graduate school. She was like no other—beautiful, smart, and strong. We started dating and within a few months, we were married. How could life get any better? I had not only found "God's perfect companion" for me, but I now had a constant source of encouragement, acceptance and validation or so I thought. I would eventually discover that my insatiable need for validation placed unrealistic expectations and pressure on my wife that were never her responsibility to carry.

God eventually placed us in an incredible church where I had the privilege of being the lead pastor. The church began to grow, lives were being changed, and God's blessings were abundant and clear. As the church grew, so did the pressures of life and ministry. My wife and I traveled through an extremely deadly cancer diagnosis, three miscarriages, birthing and raising three children, various surgeries due to the lingering effects of the car wreck earlier in life, and pastoring a growing church with multiple locations and 30-40 staff members. Any combination of these provided enough pressure to test the strongest of people and gradually, they began to reveal cracks in my faulty assumptions and foundation. I eventually started searching for ways to quiet that old familiar voice of rejection. This led to periods of "binging" on pornography and masturbation and fantasizing about ladies finding me attractive. I knew in my heart that these actions would gradually take me farther than I ever intended to go, but I continued to buy the lies—"It's just fantasy! I'm not acting on anything! It's a good release for me and it's not hurting anyone!" Each lie blurred the lines a little more until I reached a place where I was seriously considering things that I had promised I would never do.

With an unyielding appetite and need for validation and a refusal to allow Jesus Christ to be the sole source for meeting that need, I was on a collision course with choices that would devastate the heart of my wife and family and cause me to forfeit everything that I had worked so hard to accomplish. When a much younger, attractive employee started flirting with and affirming me, it wasn't long before we were having sex in my office at the church that I pastored. The affair lasted four to five months until it was fully discovered the night my wife went through my phone. Because of my betrayal, I had to relinquish my nearly 25-year tenure as lead pastor and step away from vocational ministry altogether, I lost many of my friendships and relationships on the staff and in the church, I forfeited a very generous salary and was forced to start a new career in my 50s, and the list continues. As difficult as each of these have been, they pale in comparison to the pain, heartache, and devastation I caused my wife.

Watching my wife grieve and experience this level of trauma and heartache has been the most difficult journey of my life. I absolutely abhor the choices that I made and I can never be thankful for what I did. Yet, in the midst of such anguish, God has continued to show himself faithful. He has taken the ashes of my destructive actions and is fashioning something beautiful from them. My wife and I both decided to do the hard work of recovery and healing, which includes individual counseling, groups, and mentors. After attending a local group for sexual addiction, I heard about Mark Denison and his resources in the field of sexual trauma and addiction. I purchased his book, *Jesus and the 12 Steps*, and was so encouraged and challenged by it that I reached out to Mark and Beth's ministry, There's Still Hope, for additional resources.

Shortly thereafter, I joined one of the many groups Mark leads and have met with this group weekly for over a year. In the nearly two years since my discovery, God has used my counselor, this group of men, Mark, and others to bring healing to my marriage and restoration to my soul. Through them, I realized that discovering the root of my unwanted sexual behaviors was much more important and critical than simple behavior modification and control. Focusing on the things that drive these behaviors has given me greater insight into potential wounds and deficiencies buried deep within my heart and soul and how I can find the kind of healing that prevents these unwanted behaviors in the future.

Broken Vessels

Steven

While I was raised going to church, I didn't truly surrender my life to Jesus until I was in college. I had started abusing alcohol in my high school years, and then was introduced to marijuana in college. Things progressed very quickly from there, as I began experimenting with more illicit drugs. I eventually got to the place where I realized I couldn't stop on my own. It was at this time that I met a Christian who shared the Gospel with me. It didn't take long before I took a step of faith and surrendered my life to Jesus. My desire for alcohol and drugs was taken away immediately and I rejoiced in the new freedom I had in Christ!

However, there was an area of my life in which a desire did not go away, lust and pornography.

I had been introduced to pornography at an early age, about nine years old. This was before I even knew what masturbation was, but soon after, the two quickly became intertwined.

From that time on, looking at a *Playboy* magazine seemed to be "normal," since everyone I knew was doing the same thing.

However, when I became a Christian, it became apparent that this was, in fact, sin. I tried to stop, and could even go a week or two without acting out before falling back into the same old patterns. As time went on, I was able to go months, even up to six months at one point. Yet, it would always resurface.

Then came the internet and personal computers. Pornography suddenly became even easier to access and extremely easy to hide. This pattern continued in my life, even as a Christian. Even as a ministry leader. Even as a pastor. I felt alone and powerless in this struggle. And yet, I could get on a "streak of success" long enough to convince myself that I could overcome this area of weakness and sin on my own.

Yet I would always fall back into the same old patterns again and again.

I even convinced myself that my sin wasn't *that* bad, since I never spent money on pornography, or lived out any fantasies by pursuing relationships with other people. While I acknowledged the lust in my heart, I never sought out anything beyond pornography and masturbation. I kept it all inside, contained in a tiny compartment in my heart.

I was not able to truly begin recovery until I found an accountability group comprised of pastors. Only pastors. I finally felt I had a safe place to talk and share my struggle. As a pastor, this enabled me to start processing how I had gotten to where I was in this struggle and to begin to find a path out of it. To hear the struggles and successes of other pastors who had gotten victory and walked in sobriety for over a year gave me great hope.

In this pastor's accountability group, I learned practical steps for gaining sobriety and victory. I learned boundaries that I could put in place to keep me from tripping up. I realized how much I had made provision for my flesh, to fulfill its lusts (Romans 13:14). But with better boundaries in place, I learned to be more watchful when I was lonely, angry, tired, down, depressed, or bored.

With additional help from a counselor, I learned how to overcome my hurts and wounds from my past, as they were a real source for why I continually used pornography and masturbation to bring relief.

I learned that at the core of sexual sin, there is usually an intimacy wound. Now when I struggle, I understand why and I'm more equipped to process that pain. My intimacy wounds are healing, and I'm learning how to trust the Lord with my whole being. I have finally begun to find recovery.

I have come to understand that this isn't something you can just read or pray your way out of. It takes a level of surrender of yourself, complete honesty with the Lord, and a few "safe people" to walk through it with you.

There is hope. There is lasting freedom. But you won't find it alone, with "just you and Jesus." Breaking isolation and learning to ask for help is where trust is built and freedom is found. Though the journey is difficult, I'm now walking in honesty and vulnerability, with integrity and purity.

Reggie

My first exposure to pornography was at the age of eight. I can still recall those images in my mind today. It all began when an assistant coach quietly targeted a few boys on the team, providing us with unlimited pornography and encouraging us to masturbate. What began as an innocent curiosity led to a daily habit, then to a twenty-year addiction fueled by easy access to adult material and sexual encounters.

Raised in a Christian home, I received a call into ministry my junior year in high school, but deep inside there was a war raging between my desire to follow Jesus and the need to fill my sexual addiction. In college, I experienced a few, short-lived seasons of sobriety, only to relapse and fall deeper into the addiction. By the time I graduated and began full-time ministry, I was a full-blown addict, secretly visiting massage parlors, adult bookstores and picking up prostitutes.

My life was out of control—a pastor by day and a sex addict at night. It all caught up with me in my mid-twenties when I was hospitalized and diagnosed with exhaustion and severe depression. God graciously used that rock-bottom experience to get my attention and reset my life. I began sexual addiction therapy, processed many childhood hurts, and for the first time acknowledged that my early exposure to porn and masturbation was actually sexual abuse.

Two years later, believing I had recovered, I quickly jumped into a relationship with a woman I would marry. Within the first year, it became obvious that neither of us were healthy and the marriage imploded. I soon relapsed again. By the age of thirty, I recognized my need for more structure and accountability, so I began attending a local Celebrate Recovery Ministry. CR offered me a safe place to continue to process my addiction with a group of like-minded people who were also seeking freedom. I attended weekly meetings, worked my 12-Step program and sought the counsel of my sponsor. Completely breaking the addiction was difficult with a few relapses along the way, but as I experienced genuine sobriety, I found myself hungry for more.

By my early thirties, I was living sober and knowing true freedom. It was amazing. In my late thirties, I met my current wife. However, creating a relationship not colored by addiction and sexual brokenness was new for me, so we took our time, processed our pasts together and allowed a deep, authentic friendship to develop. Now, I am 50, and am helping other men break the stronghold of pornography and sexual addiction. Walking in freedom requires me to come alongside others to do the same. I have also discovered that while I would not want to go back and relive my past, I also would not change it. My brokenness has been a tether holding me to Jesus, allowing me to experience the depths of his love and the power in sharing that relationship with others. Today, I can honestly say, "I am grateful" for the life he has given me and I surrender my story to however he desires to use it.

Tim

For the first 15 years of my life, I did not follow Jesus. I rarely attended church and had no understanding of the Bible. My mother and I began to follow Jesus when I was 15 years old. As I grew spiritually, physically, and mentally, I faced many struggles and temptations, some over which I found victory and others I did not. I married my high school sweetheart at 19 and then followed the Lord's call to ministry at 22.

A few years ago, my wife and I agreed to help a 20-year-old lady who was in college and struggling with family, financial and faith issues. All of our children were grown, married, and living in their own homes. So, after a conversation with her, we agreed to open our home and family to her. My wife and I have been married for 30-plus years and have a great relationship. We loved being married, as well as being parents and grandparents. We hoped that our family would have a positive godly impact on this young lady's life. I had pastored for more than 25 years, and we had our own routines and activities. She fit into those routines and activities very quickly. Thus, over the next two years she became a part of our family, celebrating birthdays, holidays and joining in the family photos. We even began to feel like she was family, with evening talks about the day, dating, marriage, and dreams for the future.

At church I interacted with women with clear boundaries. I wouldn't be alone with a woman other than my wife, and my office had windows to the outside of the church and into the main hallway. If conversations turned to sexual problems, I would direct the women to other ladies within the church, whom I felt would give godly counsel. Still, like many pastors, I heard stories of relational pain and heartache. I was easily able to separate these stories from myself and had little to no temptation with sexual thoughts about these women. I was comfortable giving godly counsel and/or redirecting women to other counselors.

However, those boundaries were not kept with the lady in our home. Because I officed from home several days a week and her schedule gave her hours of free time in the middle of the day, we would often find ourselves talking about her life struggles. Over time these conversations became more personal, including talks about past sexual behavior. My problem was that instead of recognizing how these behaviors had hurt her and seeking to help her find healing, I began fantasizing about them.

For most of my life porn had been something I had looked at here and there; it was not a regular part of my life. In fact, I often went years without viewing porn. I would stumble across it while doing some web search, and it would pique my interest. I would occasionally look, but soon felt convicted and turned away. I would confess this to my accountability partners and move on. But now I found myself fantasizing about this woman's story, and I began to seek porn that would demonstrate these fantasies. Soon, that was not enough.

One day, I thought of a way I could watch the young lady while she was undressing. I tried it and it worked. At first, it left me with a great sense of shame and guilt. However, after a few days my mind would drift back to seeing her again and I would do it again, taking pictures of her. Each time I would look briefly at the pictures and then felt ashamed and guilt-ridden and would delete the pictures. I would repent one day and then do it again the next. This continued for several months. I became more and more ashamed of myself, but I would keep returning to what I had a love/hate relationship with. Finally, the Lord brought my sin to light, and I was confronted by my wife and daughter. I soon lost my ministry and was charged with a crime. I was given five years' probation and deferred adjudication.

After two years of working through my court and probation counseling groups, a leader in my denomination reached out to me. His goal was to help me find the way to reconciliation and restoration within my denomination. As I began this process it led me to Mark Denison, with There's Still Hope. Through Mark's ministry, the Lord has helped me find forgiveness and hope in Jesus, as well as a spiritually healthy way to renew my mind, and today have victory over temptations that come my way. The images and feeling of the past still tempt me, however. There's Still Hope has given me some helpful practical teaching that has allowed the Holy Spirit's self-control to work in my life. Once I thought my whole life, spiritually and relationally, was destroyed and lost forever. Yet, today, I have hope in Jesus and his future for me. He is restoring my marriage, my family, my friendships, and my ministry. They look different today, but There's Still Hope!

Anthony

I was raised in a Christian family from the time I was a baby, going to church every week, hosting cell groups at our house. I became an usher at church as soon as I was big enough to hold a door open. When I was eight, I was baptized in the Holy Spirit. Over the years, I saw amazing manifestations of the power of God in my life and others around me. As a teenager I became a leader at my church and, years later, a pastor. I reached hundreds and discipled dozens, and led them to experience deep manifestations of the presence of God. I led large groups of leaders and organized massive evangelical events. However, I was very broken deep inside and was not even aware how badly. I remember so many times asking myself why God insisted on using me for his kingdom when I lacked integrity in my personal life.

Growing up in a godly home not only exposed me to an amazing God; it also exposed me to the most dangerous darkness when I found pornography on the television at the early age of 12. This exposure, combined with the divorce of my parents and different crises that developed during puberty, formed the beginning of my addiction. It was a disgusting and unwanted behavior that I managed to keep a secret for decades. I got married and never told my wife about this, damaging my vows to her. I believed the common lie that it would go away with marriage; it didn't. I thought it would go away through prayer; it didn't. I thought it would go away with me trying really hard; it didn't. I returned over and over to this unhealthy and damaging behavior. I became less present with my family and more abrasive to them. In order to hide my addiction from my wife I became verbally abusive to her, making her feel afraid to ask me about my use of pornography.

During a very stressful season when I was in constant discomfort due to different situations in life, and also full of entitlement feelings, this hidden addiction became worse and worse. I thought it wasn't too bad because it helped me to feel better, again, an entitled feeling, until finally my wife started to suspect something, and finally caught me.

When this happened, I saw the huge damage that I caused her and myself. I saw the pain and trauma that I created in her. Everything was shaken in my life. I had finally arrived at rock bottom. I started facing all the destruction that I caused in my marriage, family, ministry, and most importantly, my relationship with God.

For more than two decades of secret addiction, I never read or heard about any literature or ministry that could help me to stop, because I didn't really try. I only tried by myself in my own strength, and obviously always failed.

When I saw my life was shaken and my marriage was in danger, I started to look for help and discovered ministries, podcasts, literature, therapists and different resources that could help me. Among them, I found Mark's ministry, There's Still Hope. I joined one of his groups, and for the first time in my life, I showed my face to more than a dozen people and revealed my shameful secrets and confessed my addiction. Mark guided me, with his 90-day program, through a journey of recovery where I found freedom and experienced a totally new dimension of the amazing grace of God.

As of this writing, I am 224 days sober and free from pornography and masturbation. My relationship with Jesus is deeper and stronger than ever before. I am not tempted to go back to acting out anymore.

I am also still attending two groups every week. Every day, I have a devotional time focused on my recovery. Every day, I read material and listen to podcasts related to pornography and sex addiction, and periodically I check my progress with Mark and other men on the same path of recovery.

I stopped my unwanted behaviors, but most importantly, I have changed my attitude and my way of thinking, and I walked out of secrecy and walked into a community of people in recovery.

Today, I enjoy life so much more. I am more present with my wife, kids, and disciples. My goal is to stay sober for the rest of my life, and I will get there one day at a time, surrendering EVERYTHING to God (something easy to preach from our pulpits, but very hard to practice in our private lives). I think I can be more useful for the Kingdom over the next few years, now that I am a man of integrity today.

Isaac

My sex addiction started when I was in the sixth grade. Forty years later I finally started recovery. At first I didn't understand what I was doing. Looking back, as I grew older the tension of what really felt good and helped me escape from the world of my hurts/rejection versus knowing what was right became a constant struggle. I grew up in a Christian family who loved me but wasn't able to help me with my addiction. "I just needed to stop," I told myself. God just wanted me to do right all the time and if I didn't, then he was going to be angry until I straightened up. But I couldn't stay "good" all the time. Acting out was a place I wanted to go back to time and time again. There wasn't a safe place to tell my story. And my story was the worst of anyone's—

not only did I like pornography and masturbating; I was a crossdresser. There wasn't any worse sin—so the enemy told me.

My binge/purge cycle became a regular part of my life along with hiding clothes, isolation, lying, manipulation and deception. I would only purge out of guilt and shame, but the urges to go right back to it was always with me. I used most women in my life. I met my second wife soon after the failure of my first marriage of less than a year with several affairs mixed in. At this point, I was pretty much out of control and looked for love and acceptance wherever I could find it. I was even working in a church at this point and going to seminary. But divorce and then later discovery of one of my affairs really made my world crash in on itself. I was never approached by anyone to ask if I needed help. I was all on my own and was pretty much out of control until I met my second wife.

I really thought she was my "savior," but from the beginning I lied to her and didn't tell her anything about any of my sexual struggles. We started having sex, got pregnant and got married. I was good at the beginning, but eventually I gave into my urges and started buying clothing under my wife's nose. After several years of the guilt/shame, I finally told her about my crossdressing struggle. That started us on a never-ending cycle of hurt and pain. Many times she would find clothes that I would hide, and she would confront me. One time I finally got help through an online ministry. I told my mentor about my crossdressing, but this was to a faceless person over the internet. My wife thought this was the turning point for me. But it wasn't, as loneliness hit me again, along with isolation. I started a long slide toward finally acting out. I crushed my wife, and she told me that she was "done." She said, "You go do whatever you want to." Twenty-four years of marriage were gone and we divorced—all because of my sexual sin. I finally dropped my hidden bomb on my family, hitting everyone with shrapnel.

If God didn't take my wife from me, I wouldn't have ever started recovery. God used that as a catalyst to help me do something that I NEVER had done except with my wife—tell someone face to face about my crossdressing and that I needed help. I told a pastor about my crossdressing and did not receive any hatred or condemnation. Being willing to trust God's protection in my life was the beginning of my journey of healing. For the first time in my life, I had the feeling of connecting with God as my Father. Also, for the first time EVER, I purged ANYTHING that would cause me to have illicit thoughts in my mind. God has blessed me with having daily miracles of sobriety and just as importantly, dealing with my wounds. He has connected me with men. Most every man in my life knows my story, and, other than one exception, I have not had a negative experience—only love and care. I did have a slip, but the Holy Spirit asked me if I wanted to have that barrier between God and myself again. I didn't, so I purged and confessed to my brothers. He taught me that I needed another level of help and that is when I reached out to Mark Denison, and There's Still Hope. He walked me through his 90-day intensive program and then I joined one of his Freedom Groups. Though my two-year journey of healing is only at the beginning of where God is taking me, I wouldn't have it any other way. Trust, honesty and safety have changed my life.

Michael

Before recovery, I was obsessed with acting out. I underestimated my prior sexual struggles. I thought I was stronger than I truly was. I was ignorant of the power of sexual sin. I didn't consider myself to have a big problem with a disordered sexuality until I started acting out in the most bizarre of ways. I blocked out my conscience in order to pursue my obsession. I pursued my acting out diligently. I thought about my fantasies and then planned how I could make them happen. I can't believe how far my addiction took me. Life felt out of control. I risked my marriage and my ministry. I began to do things which I knew were wrong and went against my faith and convictions. I wanted to stop but I felt like I had to keep acting out. I lied and I hid my behaviors from my wife and my friends. I lived a double life. I acted out with porn and visited massage parlors regularly in order to act on my fantasies. I felt terrible and yet I still returned to these same behaviors. My relationship with God was inauthentic.

I found recovery by confessing my sins. Although I wasn't honest at first, I came to a point where I had to come clean. I joined a Sex Addicts Anonymous group and began to hear from others who were suffering from addiction. I began working on the 12 Steps with the support of a sponsor. I reached out to other people in groups, too. I found the There's Still Hope ministry, and thankfully joined one of their groups. It has been a tremendous support to me as I got to work through a wonderful workbook on recovery, and also discussed with others who, like me, were seeking to become men of integrity. I have been slowly learning about the root causes of my addiction. I realized that shame was a big deal in my life, and I began to address feelings of worthlessness by meditating on how God sees me. One of the things that has helped me is learning to be more in tune with my emotions. Realizing that I ran to my addiction as a coping mechanism from my past and present painful emotions has been important. I now seek to engage with my painful emotions and surrender them to God.

I now feel more at peace. I'm learning to rest in God each day. Even though I still struggle, I am in a more stable place. I now can empathize more with my wife as I have caused her unimaginable pain. Each day is an opportunity for me to turn my unwanted desires to God and truly trust that he will fight my battles. I have been sober from my unwanted behaviors for almost a year now. I feel freer from my unwanted behaviors, and more awake and alive to serve God and to serve others. I am deeply grateful for my wife and I desire to make amends to her. I don't want to return to the secrecy and hiding. I want integrity. I have to stay on guard each day, trusting in God's power.

John

My life before recovery was riddled with constant frustration. *Why can't I stop these behaviors? Why am I so irresistibly drawn to pornography, masturbation, flirting with, even sexting, women who aren't my wife?* I had no idea what was wrong with me. I was so overwhelmed with shame and regret. All my other friends (so I thought) had outgrown these behaviors in high school or college. But there I was—a new seminary graduate, just a few months into my first full-time ministry role, and I was entangled in sexual addiction. Sure, I wanted to stop what I was doing. But I had no idea how to.

So, I made a deal with myself and God. I'll stop these behaviors—the porn, the sexting, all the rest—and then maybe in 15 or 20 years, I'll tell my wife and my fellow pastors. Yes, I'd come clean. But at least by then I would be so far removed from my behaviors that no one could be that mad at me. Surely there was a "statute of limitations" on this stuff, right?

The only problem was that, well, tomorrow kept coming and I had no clue on earth how to follow through with the deal that I had drawn up for myself. That was until my wife discovered the "tip of the iceberg" of my acting out on my phone one day. This is what the Holy Spirit used—slowly, painfully—to usher (or drag) me and all of my mess into the light. Within two weeks of this partial discovery and my subsequent confession of all the rest, I was asked to resign from my dream job, and I entered the world of recovery with my pregnant and heartbroken wife.

Thankfully, my wife and I were immediately referred to a sex addiction recovery ministry connected with our church, as well as a C.S.A.T. My entire life had just gone up in flames, but I strangely knew that I was in just the right place. It was through this recovery process—recovery groups, a four-day intensive, and therapy—that I finally began to understand what was wrong with me. I was struggling with an addiction that emerged as a coping mechanism—an escape hatch, if you will—for me to deal with a lifetime of shame, fatherlessness, various forms of sexual abuse, and much more. I finally understood why I continually returned to the forbidden fruit of sexual sin. I was trying to escape the pain and discomfort of past and current life stressors; I was medicating the self-hate that I had for my acting out, with more euphoric and dopamine-filled forms of acting out. I was caught in an overwhelmingly viscous cycle that I wasn't even aware of.

As I write this, I am 16 months removed from my wife's discovery and my resignation from ministry. I haven't looked at porn in over a year. I have zero even remotely inappropriate relationships with other women. Best of all, I am walking in the light on a day-to-day basis with my wife and about a dozen trustworthy men. I am no longer baffled and clueless at my behavior. I intimately understand my triggers, and I know exactly what my on-going sexual temptations are attempting to medicate. My life is nowhere near back to normal; my wife and I struggle daily to pick up the pieces of my betrayal. But we are doing all that we know to do. We are still in therapy and are seeking the support of friends and family as we need. I have yet to return to full-time ministry, but I long for the day when the Lord opens that door again.

The road out of sexual addiction is a long and treacherous one, but I wouldn't trade it for any of my past behaviors. It is worth it because the God who refuses to waste his children's pain will use even our worst and most embarrassing mistakes to further his kingdom and bring light and freedom to those walking in darkness.

CONCLUSION

Kintsugi.

The Japanese have created an interesting art called Kintsugi. Simply said, Kintsugi is the art of restoring broken pottery pieces with gold. The practice is built on the idea that by embracing flaws and imperfections, one can create an even stronger, more beautiful piece of art. Every break is unique; instead of repairing the broken vessel like new, this 400-year-old technique actually highlights the scars and chips as part of the design.

When a pastor becomes a broken vessel, his first response is despair. His ministry may well be over. Life as he knew it is certainly over. He sees no way out. His life is in ruins, a pile of broken fragments. Putting Humpty Dumpty together again seems impossible.

And it's true. Life as he knew it is no more. But here's the big surprise—*life can actually get better*! If that sounds too good to be true, I get it. I once sat where you sit. I will never forget that Friday afternoon when I sat across the table from six men in my church, each of whom had read my clinical disclosure, which I had written for my wife and therapist one year earlier. Someone had hacked my computer, discovered the document, then passed it on to some of these men.

These well-meaning men did two things. They asked for my resignation, and they offered me immediate therapy. The therapist—whom I had hired—was waiting for me in another office. The men were afraid I would do something dangerous to myself. They even insisted on driving me to my home.

Despair was my middle name. What I didn't know, however, was that just as my jar was shattered into unrecognizable bits, the Master Designer was already planning for my Kintsugi moment. And my personal Kintsugi process continues to this day.

The key for me was to let go of my ministry and take hold of my recovery. My mentor in recovery, Dr. Milton Magness, reminded me often that nothing else matters if my recovery is not intact. So pastor, see yourself as a broken vessel in need of your own Kintsugi experience. Life can be better than ever, and you can be a better man, husband, and father in the future than you ever would have been had this addiction not taken you down in the first place.

Never see your Kintsugi process as finished. Never stand still in your recovery. In their signature book, *Real Hope, True Freedom*, Milton Magness and Marsha Means give us a great analogy for anyone who desires lasting recovery.[1] Imagine a motorboat with the drain plug pulled out. If the boat is stationary, water immediately starts to fill the boat and, if enough accumulates, the boat will sink. The amazing thing about the sinking boat is how quickly the situation can be remedied. Crank the motor and take off across the water and water will stop leaking into the boat. Moreover, the water that is already in the boat will run out of the drain hole. Sex addicts can get their lives back on track again by engaging in those activities that propel them forward.

Pastor, know that you are not alone. Your shattered vessel is not the end. What you see as a set-back is God's set-up to a future you can't imagine. The Japanese call it Kintsugi. God calls it grace.

NOTES

Introduction

1. Brinks.com.
2. Stastista.com, 2009.
3. www.yearbookofchurches.org.
4. National Congregational Study Survey, http://sites.duke.edu.
5. Samuel Smith, "Porn in the Pew: How Churches Should Help Members Dealing with Addiction," Christian Post, March 26, 2020. https://www.christianpost.com/news/porn-in-the-pew-how-churches-should-help-members-dealing-with-addiciton.html.
6. Gerald May, Addiction and Grace (New York: Harper & Row, 1988), 14.

Chapter 1

1. Joe Dallas, The Game Plan: The Men's 30-Day Strategy for Attaining Sexual Purity. (Nashville, TN: Thomas Nelson Publishing, 2005), 4.
2. "How to Deal with Addiction to Pornography," Josh McDowell, Reasonable Faith Conference, Singapore, May 2, 2018, saltandlight.org.
3. SEMrush analytics firm, data from the SEMrush Traffic analytics tool, on fightthenewdrug.org.
4. Paul J. Wright, Robert S. Tokunaga, and Ashley Kraus, "A Meta-Analysis of Pornography Consumption and Actual

Acts of Sexual Aggression in General Population Studies," Journal of Communication 66, no. 1 (February 2016), 183-205.
5. Elena Martellozzo, Andrew Monaghan, Joanna Ruth Adler, Rodolfo Leyva, "'I Wasn't Sure It was Normal to Watch It...' A Quantitative and Qualitative Examination of the Impact of Online Pornography on the Values, Attitudes, Beliefs, and Behaviors of Children and Young People," London Middlesex University (2016).
6. Pornhub Analytics, fightthenewdrug.org, December 17, 2019, "Pornhub's Annual Report."
7. Pornhub Analytics, fightthenewdrug.org, December 17, 2019, "Pornhub's Annual Report."8.
8. Ron DeHaas, January 19, 2016, covenanteyes.com.
9. "The Most Viewed Porn categories of 2017 Are Pretty Messed Up," Fight the New Drug. https://fightthenewdrug.org/pornhub-reports-most-viewed-porn-of-2017/.
10. Bill Tancer, Click: What Millions of People Are Doing Online and Why It Matters (New York: Hyperion, 2008).
11. "The Most Viewed Porn Categories of 2017 Are Pretty Messed Up," Fight the New Drug. https://fightthenewdrug.org/pornhub-reports-most-viewed-porn-of-2017.
12. "Internet Pornography by the Numbers: A Significant Threat to Society," Webroot Smarter Cybersecurity. https://www.webroot.com/us/en/resources/tips-articles/internet-pornography-by-the-numbers.
13. Nathaniel M. Lambert, Sesen Negash, Tyler F. Stillman, Spencer B. Olmstead, Frank D. Fincham, "A Love That Doesn't Last: Pornography Consumption and Weakened Commitment to One's Romantic Partner." Journal of Social and Clinical Psychology, 31, No. 4 (2012), 410-438.
14. Matt Richtel, "For pornographers, Internet's virtues turn to vices," New York Times, June 2, 2007. http://www.nytimes.com/2007/06/02/technology/02porn.html.
15. Jill Manning, "Hearing on pornography's impact on marriage & the family," U.S. Senate Hearing: Subcommittee on the Constitution, Civil rights and Property Rights, Committee on Judiciary, Nov. 10, 2005. https://www.

judiciary.senate.gov/imo/media/doc/manning testimony.11_10_05.pdf.
16. Dolf Zillmann, "Influence of unrestrained access to erotica on adolescents' and young adults' dispositions toward sexuality," Journal of Adolescent Health 27 (Aug. 2000), 41-44.
17. Jonathan Dedmon, "Is the Internet bad for your marriage? Online affairs, pornographic sites playing greater role in divorces." Press Release from the Dilenschneider Group, Inc., Nov. 14, 2002. http://www.prnewswire.com/news-releases/is-the-internet-bad-for-your-marriage-online-affairs-pornographic-sites-playing-greater-role-in-divorces-76826727.html.
18. Josh McDowell Ministry, The Porn Phenomenon: The Impact of Pornography in the Digital Age (Ventura, CA: Barna Group, 2016).
19. Chiara Sabina, Janis Wolak, and David Finkelhor, "The nature and dynamics of Internet pornography exposure for youth," CyberPsychology and Behavior, 11 (2008), 691-693.
20. Jason S. Carroll, Laura M. Padilla-Walker, Larry J. Nelson, Chad D. Olson, Carolyn McNamara Barry, and Stephanie D. Madsen, "Generation XXX: Pornography acceptance and use among emerging adults. Journal of Adolescent Research, 23 (2008), 6-30.
21. Michael Leahy, Porn University: What College Students Are Really Saying About Sex on Campus (Chicago: Northfield Publishing, 2009).
22. Barna Group, 2014 Pornography Survey and Statistics.
23. Michael Leahy, Porn @ Work: Exposing the Office's #1 Addiction (Chicago: Northfield Publishing, 2009).
24. Message Labs monthly report from March 2004, Michael Leahy, Porn @ Work.
25. Proven Men Porn Survey (conducted by Barna Group), https://www.provenmen.org/2014PornSurvey/.
26. McDowell, The Porn Phenomenon.
27. Stack, Wasserman, and Kern, "Adult Social Bonds."
28. Marnie C. Ferree, No Stones, 2nd ed. (Downers Grove, Ill: IVP Books, 2010), 71.

29. HealthyMind.com statistics for 2003; see www.healthymind.com/s-porn-stats.
30. McDowell, The Porn Phenomenon.
31. Christine J. Gardner, "Tangled in the worst of the web: What Internet porn did to one pastor, his wife, his ministry, their life," Christianity Today, March 5, 2001. http://www.christianitytoday.com/ct/2001/march5/1.42.html?paging=off.
32. Leadership Journal, "Leadership Survey."
33. Verena Klein, Tanja Jurin, Peer Briken, and Aleksander Stulhofer, "Erectile Dysfunction, Boredom, and Hypersexuality among Coupled Men from Two European Countries." The Journal of Sexual Medicine, 12, no. 11 (2015), 2160-167.
34. K. Sutton, "Patient Characteristics by Type of Hypersexuality Referral: A Quantitative Chart Review of 115 Consecutive Male Cases." Journal of Sex and Marital Therapy, 41, no. 6 (September 2, 2014), 563-80.
35. Valerie Voon, Thomas B. Mole, Paula Banca, Laura Porter, Laurel Morris, Simon Mitchell, Tatyana Lapa, Judy Karr, Neil A. Harrison, Marc N. Potenza, Michael Irvine, "Neural Correlates of Sexual Cue Reactivity in Individuals with and without Compulsive Sexual Behaviours." PLoS One, 9(7), e102419 (July 11, 2014); Daisy J. Mechelmans, Michael Irvine, Paula Banca, Laura Porter, Simon Mitchell, Tom B. Mole, Tatyana Lapa, Neil A. Harrison, Marc N. Potenza, Valerie Voon, "Enhanced Attentional Bias towards Sexually Explicit Cues in Individuals with and without Compulsive Sexual Behaviours," PLoS One, 9(8), e105476 (August 25, 2014).
36. Sheri Madigan, Anh Li, Christina L. Rash, Joris Van Ouystel, and Jeff R. Temple, "Prevalence of Multiple Forms of Sexting Behavior Among Youth: A Systematic Review and Meta-Analysis," JAMA Pediatrics, 172:4 (2018), 327-335, https://jamanetwork.com/journals/jamapediatrics/article-abstract/2673719?redirect=true.
37. University of Kent, "Research Finds a Majority Endorsing Revenge Porn," Phys.org, March 2, 2017. https://phys.org/news/2017-03-majority-endorsing-revenge-porn.html#jCp.

38. McDowell, The Porn Phenomenon.
39. "Don't send me that pic," Plan International Australia and Our Watch. https://www.plan.org.au/learn/who-we-are/blog/2016/03/02/dont-send-me-that-pic.
40. Jill Manning, "Hearing on pornography's impact on marriage & the family," U.S. Senate Hearing: Subcommittee on the Constitution, Civil Rights and Property Rights, Committee on Judiciary, Nov. 10, 2005. http://www.judiciary.senate.gov/imo/media/doc/manning_testimony_11_10_05.pdf.
41. Dolf Zillmann and Jennings Bryant, "Effects of massive exposure to pornography," in Pornography and Sexual Aggression (New York: Academic Press, 1984), 560-578.
42. Vincent Cyrus Yoder, Thomas B. Virden III, and Kiran Amin, "Internet Pornography and Loneliness: An Association?" Sexual Addiction & Compulsivity, 12 (2005), 19-44.
43. Michele L. Ybarra and Kimberly J. Mitchell, "Exposure to Internet Pornography among Children and Adolescents: A National Survey." CyberPsychology & Behavior, 8 (2005), 473-486.
44. Jochen Peter and Patti M. Valkenburg, "Adolescents' exposure to a sexualized media environment and their notions of women as sex objects," Sex Roles, 56 (2007), 381-395.
45. Elizabeth M. Morgan, "Association between young adults' use of sexually explicit materials and their sexual preferences, behaviors, and satisfaction," Journal of Sex Research, 48 (2011), 520-530.
46. Katie Szittner, "Study exposes secret world of porn addiction," Sydney.edu. May 10, 2012. http://sydney.edu.au/news/84.html?newsstoryid=9176.
47. Jill Manning, "Hearing."
48. Dolf Zillman and Jennings Bryant, "Effects of massive exposure to pornography," in Pornography and Sexual Aggression (New York: Academic Press, 1984): Dolf Zillman and Jennings Bryant, "Shifting preferences in pornography consumption," Communication Research 13 (1986); 560-578, Dolf Zillman and Jennings Bryan, "Pornography's impact on

sexual satisfaction," Journal of Applied Social Psychology 18 (1988): 438-453, Dolf Zillman and Jennings Bryant, "Effects of Prolonged Consumption of Pornography on Family Values," Journal of Family Issues 9 (1988): 518-544.
49. Vincent Cyrus Yoder, Thomas B. Virden III, and Kiran Amin, "Internet Pornography and Loneliness: An Association?" Sexual Addiction & Compulsivity, 12 (2005), 19-44.
50. Manning, "Hearing."
51. Ibid.
52. Christina Mancini, Amy Reckenwald, and Eric Beauregard, "Pornographic exposure over the life course and the severity of sexual offenses: Imitation and cathartic effects," Journal of Criminal Justice, 40 (2012), 21-30.
53. Martin Monto, Focusing on the Clients of Street Prostitutes: A Creative Approach to Reducing Violence Against Women, Report submitted to the U.S. Department of Justice, Oct. 30, 1999. https://www.ncjrs.gov/pdffiles1/nij/grants/182859.pdf.
54. Janet Hinson Shoppe, "When words are not enough: The search for the effects of pornography on abused women," Violence Against Women, 10 (2004), 56-72.
55. Ana Bridges, Robert Wosnitzer, Chyng Sun, and Rachel Liberman, "Aggression and sexual behavior in best-selling pornographic videos: A content analysis update," Violence Against Women, 16 (Oct. 2010), 1065-1085.

Chapter 2

1. Sam Louie, "Pastors and Porn," Psychology Today, January 30, 2020.
2. Ed Stetzer, "Six Ways Pastors Struggle: You Are Not Alone," November 15, 2019. https://www.christianitytodaycom/edstetzer/2019/november/six-ways-pastors-struggle-you-are-not-alone.html.
3. Ibid.
4. Chantelle Pattemore, "10 Ways to Build and Preserve Better Boundaries," June 2, 2012. https://psychcentral.com/lib/10-way-to-build-and-preserve-better-boundaries.

5. Stetzer, "Six Ways Pastors Struggle: You Are Not Alone."
6. Hershael York, "10 Challenges Every Pastor Will Face," Southern Baptist Seminary, October 3, 2014, https://equip.sbts.edu/article.
7. Max DuPree, "3 Roles Every Leader Must Play," https://www.modernservantleader.com/servant-leadership/3-roles-every-leader-must-play/.
8. Thom Rainer, "Eight of the Most Significant Struggles Pastors Face," March 1, 2014. (Church Answers Featuring Thom Rainer) https://churchanswers.com/blog/eight-of-the-most-significant-struggles-pastors-face/.
9. Ryan Howes, "Who Doesn't Need Therapy?" Psychology Today, July 1, 2014. https://www.psychologytoday.com/us/blog/in-therapy/201407/who-doesnt-need-therapy.
10. Darin Shaw, "5 Benefits of Christian Counseling," June 6, 2018. https://www.honeylake.clinic/5-benefits-of-christian-counseling/.
11. Thom Rainer, "Eight of the Most Significant Struggles Pastors Face."
12. Shana Schutte, "Intimacy with God: The Way to True Fulfillment," January 1, 2009. (Focus on the Family) https://www.focusonthefamily.com/faith/intimacy-with-god-the-way-to-true-fulfillment/.

Chapter 3

1. Kenneth Berding, A Key Insight about Romans 7 from a Conversation with J.I. Packer. (La Mirada, CA: Biola University, April 4, 2012).
2. David Frost, Prime Time Live TV Special. (PBS, February 3, 1993).
3. Luke Gibbons, "Porn Trends," World Magazine, Vol. 30, No. 20 (October 3, 2015).
4. Ibid.
5. Mark Twain, www.twainquotes.com/Adam.html.
6. Berding, A Key Insight about Romans 7 from a Conversation with J.I. Packer.

7. Donald Grey Barnhouse, Romans. (Grand Rapids, MI: Eerdmans, 1983).
8. "Martin Luther Quotes that Still Ring True," Relevant Magazine (October 31, 2017). http://relevantmagine.com/god/18-martin-luther-quotes-still-ring-true.
9. Matthew Henry, Commentary on the Whole Bible. (Grand Rapids, MI: Zondervan Publishing, 1961).
10. www.amazon.com/When-learn-experience-scars-Charles/dp/B01MOHTCJ7.
11. Lauren Porter, "Give Me One Hundred Preachers," Porter's Progress (April 23, 2010). http://laurenporter.wordpress.com/2010/04/23/give-me-one-hundred-preachers/.
12. John Piper, Desiring God. (Sermon delivered October 13, 2012). http://www.desiringgod.org/.../god-is-most-glorified-in-us-when-we-are-most-satisfied.
13. Carey Nieuwhof, "5 Signs I Might Be Headed for a Moral Failure," https://careynieuwhof.com/5-reasons-pastors-fail-morally/.

Chapter 4

1. Lance Witt, sermoncentral.com, February 2, 2021.
2. https://www.barna.com/the-porn-phenomenon/.
3. Collin Hansen, "Pastor, Confess Your Sin—No Matter the Consequences," The Gospel Coalition, November 1, 2016, thegospelcoalition.org.
4. Arthur P. Boers, "Everyone's Pastor, No One's Friend," Christianity Today, January 1, 1991, christianitytoday.com.
5. Boers, "Everyone's Pastor, No One's Friend."
6. Arnold A. Dallimore, Spurgeon: A Biography (Carlisle, PA: Banner of Truth, 1995), 14.
7. J. B. Torre & M. D. Lieberman. Putting Feelings into Words: Affect Labeling as Implicit Emotion Regulation. Emotion Review, 2018;10(2), 116-124.
8. Y. C. Yang, C. Boen, K. Gerken, T. Li, K Schorpp, & K. M. Harris. "Social Relationships and Physiological Determinants of Longevity Across the Human Lie Span."

Proc Natl Acad Sci USA, 2016;113(3), 578-583. doi:10.1073/pnas.1511085112.
9. Joshua Reich, "Why Most Pastors Are Nice People but Don't Make Good Friends," churchplants.com.
10. J. Garrett Kell, "The Fruit of Confessing Sin," July 18, 2021, crossway.org.
11. Kell, "The Fruit of Confessing Sin."
12. Mike MacKenzie, "Confession for the Pastor," Marbleretreat.org.
13. J. Van Olphen, A. Schulz, B. Israel, et al. "Religious Involvement, Social Support, and Health among African American Women on the East Side of Detroit." J Gen Intern Med., 2003;18(7), 549-557. doi:10.1046/j.1525-1497.2003.21031.w.

Chapter 5

1. John MacArthur, "Should Fallen Pastors Be Restored?" adopted from The Master's Plan for the Church, 1991, oneplace.com.
2. Aaron Earls, "Most Pastors Agree Abuse Should Ban Them from Ministry," Lifeway Research, June 22, 2021, christianitytoday.com.
3. Jeramie Rinne, "How to Pray for Your Pastor," November 11, 2019. https://www.crossway.org.
4. John Piper, "Series: Biblical Eldership," desiringgod.org.
5. Ed Taylor, "7 Things to Consider Related to Pastors & Adultery," August 1, 2017, https://edtaylor.org/2017/08/01/7-things-to-consider-related-to-pastors-adultery/.
6. Harry Schaumburg, "Sexual Sin in the Ministry," March 6, 2012, desiringgod.org
7. Editorial Staff, "Progress, Not Perfection in Recovery," American Addiction Centers, September 24, 2020, https://alcoholrehab.com/progress-not-perfection-in-recovery.
8. Staff, AA Cleveland District Office, "The Importance of Honesty in Recovery," n.d., https://www.aacle.org/importance-of-honesty-in-recovery/.

9. Scotty Smith, "You Asked: Am I Disqualified from Ministry?" July 21, 2013, thegospelcoalition.org.
10. Garrett Kell, "Does Pornography Use Disqualify a Pastor?" (December 30, 2018), 9marks.org.
11. Joe McKeever, "Some People Are Disqualified to Serve. Here's Why," February 17, 2013, joemckeever.com.
12. Rose Sweet, "Forgiveness and Restoration," July 15, 2021, focusonthefamily.com.
13. Lillian Tryon, "Biblical Concepts of Restoration for Lifestyle Change," The Journal of Biblical Foundations of Faith and Learning, Vol. 3, Issue 1, Article 28, 2018, https://knowledge.e.souther.edu.
14. Tim Challies, "For the Pastor Knee-Deep in Immorality," Trending Topics, July 19, 2018, challis.com.
15. Martin Luther: Selections from His Writings, ed. John Dillenberger (New York: Anchor Books, 1962), 87. From a sermon preached c. 1519.
16. Ray Stedman, "Disqualified!" November 19, 1978, Ray Stedman Ministries, raystedman.org.

Chapter 6

1. Alcoholics Anonymous World Services. Alcoholics Anonymous Big Book. 4th ed. (New York: Alcoholics Anonymous World Services; 2001).
2. J. F. Kelly, R. Stout, W. Zywiak, & R. Schneider. A 3-year study of addiction mutual-help group participation following intensive outpatient treatment. Alcohol Clin Exp Res., 2006; 30(8), 1381-1392.
3. S. E. Zemore, M. Subbaraman, & J. S. Tonigan. (Involvement in 12-step activities and treatment outcomes. Substance Abuse. 2013; 3491), 41-50.
4. J. G. Woititz. The Complete ACOA Sourcebook. Deerfield Beach, FL: Health Communications, 2002.
5. Ibid.
6. Steven M. Melemis, "Relapse Prevention and the Five Rules of Recovery," September 3, 2015. The Journal of Biology

and Medicine. https://www.ncbi.nlm.nih.gov/pmc/articles/PMC4553654/.

7. Joshua S. Hill, "What It Really Means to Be Desperate for God," Relevant Magazine, July 8, 2016, https://relevantmagazine.com/what-it-really-means-to-be-desperate-for-god/.
8. Ana Menez, "What It Really Means to Be Desperate for God," 2018, https://godinterest.com/what-it-really-means-to-be-desperate-for-god/.
9. www.inspirationalchristians.org/biography/dwight-l-moody-biography.
10. George Sweeting, Who Said That? (Chicago: Moody Publishers, 1995).
11. Mark Laaser, Talking to Your Kids About Sex. (Colorado Springs, CO: WaterBrook Press, 1999).
12. Debbie Laaser, http://faithfulandture.com/product/full-disclosure.
13. Alcoholics Anonymous, 4th ed. (New York, NY: Alcoholics Anonymous World Services, Inc., 2002), 17.
14. Doug Weiss, "What Is Sex Addiction?" (Heart to Heart Counseling Center).

Chapter 7

1. http://www.huffingtonpost.com/susan-shapiro/addiction-bookb1375658.html.
2. Dr. Elizabeth Hartney, "Long-Term Strategies for Overcoming Addiction," July 24, 2020, https://www.verywellmind.com/overcoming-addiction/.
3. http://psychcentral.com/blog/archives/2010/06/05/12-ways0to-beat-addiction/.
4. Tiffany Douglass," How to Overcome an Addiction," Psychological Health, August 30, 2021, https://www.wikihow.com/how-to-overcome-an-addiction-14-steps.
5. http://psychcentral.com/blog/archives/2010/06/05/12-ways-to-beat-addiction/.
6. http://healingheartscounselingsd.com/9-tips-on-how-to-overcome-sex-addiction/.

7. "11 Recovery Tools to Help You Beat Addiction," Turnbridge, https://www.turnbridge.com/11-recovery-tools-to-help-you-beat-addiction/.
8. Lea Winerman, "Breaking Free from Addiction," Monitor, June 2013, Vol 44, No. 6, p. 30. https://www.apa.org/breaking-free-from-addiction/.
9. Marc Galanter, "Overcoming Addiction," Psychology Today, June 9, 2016. https://psychologytoday.com/overcoming-addiction.
10. John Trogdon, "10 Powerful Tips for Beating Any Kind of Addiction," Productive Club, n.d., https://productiveclub.com/how-to-overcome-any-addiction.
11. "11 Recovery Tools to Help You Beat Addiction," Turnbridge, https://www.turnbridge.com/11-recovery-tools-to-help-you-beat-addiction/.
12. Oscar Wilde, The Picture of Dorian Gray, July 1890. https://www.goodreads.com/quotes.
13. Elizabeth Grace Saunders, "Make Time for 'Me Time,'" Harvard Business Review, April 1, 2021, https://hbr.2021/04/make-time-for-me-time/.

Chapter 8

1. Steve Roll, "Four Things Pastors Should Know About Restoration," https://tonycooke.org/articles-by-others/4-things-about-restoration/.
2. S. Brown. Treating the Alcoholic. A Developmental Model of Recovery. (New York: Wiley, 1985). [Google Scholar].
3. Steven M. Melemis, "Relapse Prevention and the Five Rules of Recovery," September 3, 2015. The Journal of Biology and Medicine. https://www.ncbi.nlm.nih.gov/pmc/articles/PMC4553654/.
4. Ibid.
5. Chris Fabry, Pastoral Restoration: The Path to Recovery. https://media.focusonthefamily.com/pastoral/pdf/PAS PastoralRestoration.pdf.

6. "5 Things Addicts Convince Themselves Are True," A Journey Pure Facility, 2021, https://www.12keysrehab.com/5-things-addicts-convince-themselves-are-true/.
7. Russell Moore, "What to Do When a Pastor Falls," April 15, 2016, https://www.russellmoore.com/what-to-do-when-a-pastor-falls.
8. Ibid.

Chapter 9

1. Patrick Carnes, Out of the Shadows (Center City, MN: Hazelden, 1983), 195.
2. Nick Stumbo, "3 Guardrails that Will Change Your Life," June 6, 2019, https://puredesire.org/3-guardrails-that-will-change-your-life/.
3. Ibid.
4. George, "Overcoming Sex Addiction," Neulia Compulsion Solutions, https://www.compulsionsolutions.com/overcoming-sex-addiction/.
5. Robert Weiss, Sex Addiction 101 (Deerfield Beach, FL: Heath Communications, Inc., 2015), 127-129.
6. Brandon Kelley, "5 Pastoral Guardrails to Keep You from Falling Off the Cliff," 2016, https://www.rookiepreacher.com/5-pastoral-guardrails-to-keep-you-from-falling-off-the-cliff/.
7. Ibid.
8. Billy Graham, Just As I Am, from "On This Date: The Modesto Manifesto," October 24, 2017, www.billygrahamlibrary.org.
9. W. R. Miller, R. J. Myers, & S. Hiller-Sturmhofel. "The Community Reinforcement Approach," The Journal of the National Institute on Alcohol Abuse and Alcoholism, 1999. PubMed PMID: 10890805.
10. Andy Stanley, "Guardrails: Avoiding Regrets in Your Life," September 6, 2011, Churchwidejourney.com/guardrails/.
11. Covenanteyes.com.
12. Milton Magness, Stop Sex Addiction (Las Vegas: Central Recovery Press, 2013).

13. Steve Whitaker, "A Guardrail that Saves Lives," TFA Communications, February 16, 2017. https://thefirstacademy.org/blog.

Chapter 10

1. G.E. Vaillant, "A Long-Term Follow-Up of Male Alcohol Abuse," Arch Gen Psychiatry, 1996. 53(3), 243-9.
2. F. Kiefer, "Comparing and Combining Naltrexone and acamprosate in Relapse Prevention," Archives of General Psychiatry, January 2003.
3. N.D. Volkow, G.J. Wang, J.S. Fowler, D. Tomasi, F. Telang, "Addiction: Beyond Dopamine Reward Circuitry." (Proceedings of the National Academy of Sciences of the United States of America, September 13, 2011.) PubMed PMID: 21402948.
4. Ben Lesser, "A Discussion of the Recovery Stages and Their Importance," May 16, 2021. https://dualdiagnosis.org/a-discussion-of-the-recovery-stages-and-their-importance.
5. Lantie Elisabeth Jorandby, "How to Guard Against Relapse," January 22, 2021. https://www.psychologytoday.com/us/blog/use-your-brain/202101/how-guard-against-relapse.
6. Kristina Ackermann, "Warning Signs of Relapse: Depression, Stress, and Other Triggers," American Addiction Centers, August 4, 2021. https://americanaddictioncenters.org/warning-signs-of-relapse.
7. Ibid.
8. Adam Felman, "Why Stress Happens and How to Manage It," Medical News Today, March 12, 2020. https://medicalnewstoday.com/why-stress-happens-and-how-to-manage-it.
9. https://www.psychologytoday.com/us/basics/relapse.
10. Terrence T. Gorski, Passages Through Recovery: An Action Plan for Preventing Relapse. (Center City, MN: Hazelden Publishing, 1989).
11. J. F. Kelly, R. Stout, W. Zywiak, & R. Schneider, "A 3-Year Study of Addiction Mutual-Help Group Participation

12. S. E. Zemore, M. Subbaraman, & J. S. Tonigan, "Involvement in 12-Step Activities and Treatment Outcomes," Substance Abuse, 2013. 34(1), 60-69. 3558929.
13. Aaron Beck, F. D. Wright, C. F. Newman, & B. S. Liese. Cognitive Therapy of Substance Abuse (Guilford Press, 1993), 25.
14. Steven M. Melemis, "Relapse Prevention and the Five Rules of Recovery," The Journal of Biology and Medicine, September 3, 2015. https://www.ncbi.nlm.nih.gov/pmc/articles/PMC4553654/.
15. Amy Keller, "Alcoholic Recovery Stages," February 28, 2020. https://www.drugrehab.com.
16. "The 6 Stages of Change in Addiction Recovery," Boca Detox Center, March 21, 2019. https://www.bocadetox.com/the-6-stages-in-addiction-recovery.
17. Steven M. Melemis, "Relapse Prevention and the Five Rules of Recovery," September 3, 2015. The Journal of Biology and Medicine. https://www.ncbi.nlm.nih.gov/pmc/articles/PMC4553654/.

Chapter 11

1. Tall Prince, "Leading with a Limp," Internet Pornography: A Ministry Leader's Handbook, 2010. http://wagmunacom/flash/downloads/Covenant-Eyes-Internet-Porn.
2. Michael L. and Sharon P. Hill, "The healing of a Warrior," a Cyberbook publication, 2000, www.thedovecenter.org.
3. Cheryl Mann Bacon, "Best Practices for Dismissing a Minister," September 24, 2019, christianchronicle.org.
4. Roger Barrier, "When to Fire Your Pastor," crosswalk.com.
5. Mark Chaves, "Does Our Church Need to Hire a Consultant or Not?" (https://faithandleadership.com).
6. Jared C. Wilson, "Thoughts on the Restoration of Fallen Pastors," December 7, 2017, thegospelcoalition.org.
7. John Piper, "Is It Possible to Restore a Pastor Who Has Sinned Sexually?" April 20, 2009, desiringgod.org.

8. Miroslav Kis, "Dealing with a Fallen Pastor," 2004, ministrymagazine.org.
9. Jim Meyer, "Why Give a Terminated Pastor a Severance Package?" Restoring Kingdom Builders (February 24, 2014), https://blog.restoringkingdombuilders.org.
10. David L. Bea, "Avoiding Liability when Disciplining Pastors or Church Members," Bea & VandenBerk, Attorneys at Law, 2011, beavendenberk.com.
11. Karl Vaters, "Leading a Church Through Difficult Times," Christianity Today, February 24, 2018. https://www.christianitytoday.com.

Chapter 12

1. Diane Shirlaw-Ferreira, "God Uses Broken People—4 Reasons God Uses the Weak to Do Amazing Things," September 19, 2021, https://www.worthbeyondrubies.com/god-uses-broken-people/.

Conclusion

1. Milton Magness and Marsha Means, Real Hope, True Freedom (Las Vegas: Central Recovery Press, 2017), 235.

About the Author

Dr. Mark Denison, along with his wife Beth, is the founder of *There's Still Hope*, a recovery ministry for those who have fallen to sexual brokenness. Mark leads men through his acclaimed 90-Day Recovery course and leads seven weekly recovery groups, including one that is held specifically for pastors. Mark and Beth also lead several recovery groups for couples.

Mark serves as a Recovery Specialist for C3 Global Network, which offers resources to hundreds of churches. Additionally, Mark is a frequent speaker for Iron Sharpens Iron, Come to the Table, Castimonia, and other national conferences. Mark is the founding pastor of Recovery Church, with campuses in Florida, Texas, and online.

For over 30 years, Dr. Denison served as a senior pastor to three churches in Texas. His education includes a D.Min. (Southwestern Baptist Theological Seminary), M.Div. (SWBTS), MAHS (Liberty University), and B.A. (Houston Baptist University). Mark is also a trained PSAP (Pastoral Sex Addiction Professional), and has been trained by Celebrate Recovery. Married since 1983, Mark and Beth live in Bradenton, Florida near their son, and are proud parents to an adorable Shih-Tzu.

Other Books by Mark Denison

Life Recovery Plan	*Porn in the Pew*
Jesus & the 12 Steps	*Couples Recovery Guide*
Porn-Free in 40 Days	*90-Day Recovery Guide*
365 Days to Sexual Integrity	*52 Exercises*

www.ingramcontent.com/pod-product-compliance
Lightning Source LLC
Chambersburg PA
CBHW051101160426
43193CB00010B/1273